GIFTS IN THE RUINS

GIFTS IN THE RUINS

Rediscovering What Matters Most

ROSEMARY LULING HAUGHTON

with drawings by the author

ORBIS BOOKS

Maryknoll, New York 10545

Founded in 1970, Orbis Books endeavors to publish works that enlighten the mind, nourish the spirit, and challenge the conscience. The publishing arm of the Maryknoll Fathers and Brothers, Orbis seeks to explore the global dimensions of the Christian faith and mission, to invite dialogue with diverse cultures and religious traditions, and to serve the cause of reconciliation and peace. The books published reflect the views of their authors and do not represent the official position of the Maryknoll Society. To learn more about Maryknoll and Orbis Books, please visit our website at www.maryknoll.org.

Library of Congress Cataloging-in-Publication Data

Haughton, Rosemary.
    Gifts in the ruins : rediscovering what matters most / Rosemary Luling
  Haughton ; with drawings by the author.
      p. cm.
    ISBN 1-57075-556-6
    1. Spiritual life. I. Title.
    BL624.H348 2004
    204'.32—dc22

                                                            2004009731

Contents

Foreword

Joan Chittister

W arning label to the reader: Rosemary Haughton's *Gifts in the Ruins* is a book that does not end thinking, as many books are inclined to attempt to do. It doesn't give ironclad answers to any of life's great questions, for instance. It doesn't dogmatize or analyze or insist on the rightness of any particular action or attitude. It's not even selling anything that will make life more exciting or a career more effective or relationships more satisfying or personal development more understandable. On the contrary.

This is a book that simply begins the kind of thinking that can change lives. Yours and mine. It's not about us, of course. It's about the writer. But it is, at the same time, a challenge to the way we ourselves think. About our lives. About our own spiritual treasure-house. About what we think it means to be human. About what living is all about. Or better yet: about the way we measure life and faith and spiritual development.

In this deceptively charming book—deceptive because it seems so simple when it is really disarmingly profound; charming because it is so serious when it seems so mundane—respected theologian Rosemary Luling Haughton suspends life in midair to ask herself what it is, after long years of reflection and analysis, that gives substance and meaning to her own life now and why. She looks back over her own life at the end of a long career as a thinker-theologian and asks herself what she really values. She determines what it is that has served her best in life, given her a glimpse of the face of God in the here and now, been the best of her beliefs, the most spiritually usable of all the spiritual things she ever learned.

What's more, she not only lets us in on her answers but gives us both the freedom and a model of how to do it ourselves. We would all be well served to do what she has done.

In weaving her wreath of spiritual choices, she prods the rest of us to take a similar inventory of our own beliefs and spiritual gifts in order to define the compass points by which we steer, the foundations on which we stand. The whole enterprise is the kind of spiritual practice and discipline that has been long ignored, long needed in this world of constantly changing cultural truisms and rote religion.

Rosemary grew up in World War II Europe with all the political, social and economic consequences such an upbringing implies. She struggled through the same questions of faith most of us struggle with but in a family whose religious traditions were either missing or mixed.

She became a Catholic at the age of sixteen, married, started a family, and then found herself in the middle of the theological tensions that came out of Vatican II. And in the midst of it all, she raised her ten children (and two foster children) and did public ministry at the same time because being and doing were the hallmark of her faith. And during that time she came to feminist consciousness in a male-dominated church that was unprepared for and unwelcoming of the questions of women.

Like us, in other words, she has lived on shifting sands all her life. She has watched both the world and the church fail to make good on the kind of promises these two seemingly stable worlds once offered: certainty, security, innocence and righteousness.

She is a woman who has bought her faith at great price and with great depth and, thanks to *Gifts in the Ruins,* we are again all the richer for it.

The basic truth is that Rosemary Haughton is just like the rest of us. The one difference, if there is a difference, is that she has given great thought to the meaning of faith and spirituality every step of the way while most of us take it all for granted. While most people ritualized religion and reduced it to some kind of public routine, she thought about it. She wanted to know where the ideas came from, what they really meant to convey, how ideas that gave life to one period needed to be reinterpreted for another.

When the faith format of our childhood slips away, as it must if we are ever to become spiritually mature, the temptation is to assume that there is nothing of the spirit left in us. *Gifts* gives us the opportunity to look again at what it is we see of God in life. Or more to the point, perhaps, to recognize that there are many miracles of faith along the way in life that most of us have learned to ignore in favor of "answers" over the simple experience of becoming conscious of God in life.

This book is an excursion through consciousness that transcends "creeds" and so takes us to the point where belief really begins and where faith comes to life.

This book makes some simple but absolutely fundamental points, if we are going to live truly happy lives. Haughton is clear about all of them: We must come to understand that life is not a straight line. Life, she points out, is a series of choices because choices change from stage to stage. "Belief," she says, "is about choosing and choosing again."

Then, in the end, we may find as she has that life is one long process of coming to be amazed at what we've always taken for granted.

Life, we finally learn, is not lived in a straight line. As Søren Kierkegaard wrote, "Life is lived forward but it is understood backward."

Introduction

$\mathcal{T}$here comes a time, for many people of faith, when they look at the beliefs they have affirmed with conviction and enthusiasm and wonder what is left.

It happens to the young, who were brought up as believers, when adult experiences and questions shred the taken-for-granted certainties of childhood.

It happens to people who have faithfully struggled to live and act as believers, and discover that, almost without noticing it, the affirmations of faith now have questions attached to them. The affirmations can no longer be repeated with wholehearted, joyous confidence.

Many of these are women, whose love of their religious tradition has been eroded by dismissive attitudes, contempt for women's gifts and capabilities, by subtle and not-so-subtle sexual exploitation and subtle and not-so-subtle denigration and rejection. This erosion of faith happened to me, which is why I wrote this short book. I want to share my response to such an experience as a way forward to rediscover spiritual faith after bitterness and a sense of betrayal swamped the faith that was once so clear.

The diminishment of faith happens in different ways. For many, wholehearted commitment has been chipped away or suddenly smashed by the awareness of pervasive corruption and hypocrisy in the religious structures and the culture of secrecy that protects the system. Many have been shocked by the high-handed arrogance or callous indifference of their churches to real moral dilemmas. It can be years before it becomes clear that belief and hope have been so undermined that little is left, or disappointment may happen suddenly after some egregious act of betrayal.

Sometimes beliefs themselves have insensibly come to seem incredible, as all attempts to understand them differently, by different images, are rejected and denounced as lack of faith.

In the end, for so many and for so many reasons, nothing is left but a certain nostalgia, a few kind memories or, worse, a deep-seated anger or cynicism. And for those whose experience of religion in earlier years was harsh and dogmatic, all of religion might be dumped with relief.

For those who find themselves unable to claim the faith they once thought they held, there is a stark question to be asked: "Is anything left?" If the system of belief can no longer make sense and inspire hope, does that mean all that has been known, learned, loved, and practiced must be rejected?

To many, that seems the only honest thing to do. If the system is seen as corrupt and oppressive or the beliefs as incredible, what else can a sincere person do? To some, that rejection comes as a relief, the casting off of a hampering and unbecoming garment. To others, the rejection is deeply painful, like the loss of a dear friend.

Yet, however definite and necessary the decision to reject old systems seems, it is not possible to discard the memories, whether we want them or not. Some things linger in the mind and imagination. Faces of people whose faith was clear and attractive, customs of the seasons, hymn tunes, images of beauty in art and architecture, habits of mind that have shaped behavior. These things remain; they are part of ourselves, yet they can seem of little value because they appear inevitably linked to so much that must be rejected, that is incredible, tainted, or even evil.

Of what use are these fragile memories? They seem merely a handful of pretty flowers. Can we do more than scatter them on the grave of our hopes?

The suggestion of this short book is that, outrageously, it is these fragile things that can be the source of new life. Instead of being an image of loss they are about freedom, freshness. These remembered things that, almost reluctantly, we may still cherish can become new dis-coveries that open possibilities, become sources of strength and hope. These fragile things can give us the courage to live in harsh times and face an uncertain future. Their fragility can turn out actually to be their strength, when the great structures of organized religion crack and crumble. The fact is, we are free, anytime, to choose and claim gifts of the spirit wherever we find them. Whatever we find, anywhere, that seems to us true and good is ours for the picking. Importantly, they need not be "religious" things at all, yet they feed our spirits. Flowers flourish on garbage dumps and in bomb ruins, not just in gardens. In a world that seems better at destruction than building or planting, we need to have the vision and courage to recognize and choose life in unexpected places.

The fact is, we can pick spiritual truths wherever we find them, from old traditions or new discoveries, linking, making unexpected con-nections, and accepting these unearned gifts with amazement and grace. They come to us unattached, without strings—except that, like flowers, their roots are in the earth of our human being.

These things may be a changed recognition of older experience or new discoveries, but they are true for us because we know them by an instant recognition of some goodness, some beauty, that is there. Each is a gift, each is chosen. If there are connections, we make them. The gathering of such choices is not a sad remnant but fresh knowing and loving. These are gifts—we only have to recognize them and choose to accept them.

But what of all those people who have not become disillusioned or angry, who remain deeply committed to a spiritual tradition, who have questions and doubts, perhaps, but by and large can proclaim a creed with assurance, pride and gratitude?

As I hope to show, *all* believers actually make choices from gifts offered, whether they know it or not. They do this simply because of the natural limitations of the human mind and heart. One may assent notionally to a whole list of beliefs but, at any given time, only some of them pull at the heart, evoke feelings of amazement, satisfaction, joy, hope. The rest are just background. They may be believed to be true, in some sense, but they are not what gives energy and courage at this moment.

These things we recognize and choose are in some ways like flowers. To pick a flower is a choice—you didn't have to make it, though if a flower is offered you by a child or a lover it's hard not to accept the gift. And flowers don't last, so we need to keep on picking, keep on choosing, from the gifts that are all around us. Only while we choose does the gift remain ours.

Whether we are still committed to a tradition, or hanging onto remnants of it or scarcely touching its fringes, whether our relationship with belief is solid, or tattered by betrayal or demands to believe the unbelievable, or just evaporated by irrelevance, we can all make choices of what may seem fragile and ephemeral but is actually the stuff of love and life.

This book tries to show how and why this is true.

The first part of this book is about the nature of the spiritual choices we can make, out of the countless gifts, so lovely and so fragile, that are offered to us. These are not only those that express a religious tradition in the clear sense but more ordinary gifts which, when we really *look* at them, reveal such unexpected riches.

The longer part of the book, however, is about some of the gifts that I have personally chosen, the gifts which at this point in my life enrich and enliven and discipline and uphold me.

I have chosen to structure this short book in this very personal way simply because my chosen gifts are my own, yet linked to others. So my hope in doing this is that those who read may want to do what I have done, recognizing and pondering and choosing the gifts each one perceives and chooses, and never mind what anyone else tells you should be chosen.

Part I

Seeing and Choosing

Changing and Choosing

$\mathscr{C}$ertain moments of perception can change your life, moments when you encounter a reality that pierces, challenges, moves; you have to make a choice—to respond or to reject—and the choice shapes you from that moment.

It can be beauty, or terror, or awe, or compassion; a piece of music, a great tree, images of horror in war, the soaring arches of a cathedral, the frail courage of a child with cancer. It can be an ancient symbol—an icon, a star of David — that calls up a richness of tradition, so old, yet so new, terrible and beautiful. You may have seen it a hundred times but suddenly there's a new awareness and it breaks through your deficiencies and demands a choice.

You can choose not to respond or to respond only with a flicker of appreciation, like buying a postcard in a tourist spot. Or you can let it move you beyond where you were, into a new relation of awareness and conviction. It's frightening, because this is a real choice, a choice that involves not only changed perception but changed action. You are no longer the same.

I can think, for instance, of the men and women who join the organization Doctors Without Borders and set aside part of a normal and useful medical career to spend months in very dangerous places caring for desperately wounded or sick people, always aware of those they can't help, always with a background of fear, yet with deep satisfaction in the work. What made them choose? It wasn't a rational career choice, but something challenged and changed them.

A conversion experience is like that, a moment when a truth that was "outside" demands to become part of me. It's not always dramatic. It can seem to be quite a small change, like deciding to pay a little more for coffee that's grown by people who get paid a fair price for it, or refusing to buy clothes made in sweatshops, even if they are cheaper. But such a moment of choice can rearrange a whole life, insinuating new values, new perceptions, that upset one's life for good.

These life-giving choices may be clearly connected to religious beliefs and systems, even those we can't accept in their entirety, or (so it can seem) at all. It is very exciting to discover that some cherished memory from a religious background can be rediscovered, chosen like a fresh flower, rescued from associations that dim or distort it. If I have happy memories of Christmas, for instance, I can rediscover the delight, and the ever-new symbol of hope that is an infant—vulnerable yet triumphant, in poverty yet in intensity of love. Never mind (at least for the while) whether we feel uncomfortable with the religious descriptions or disgusted by consumer hysteria. Think, rather, of candles in windows, children's faces before the lighted tree. These things are real. They can open up an almost painful tenderness of hope. I can choose these things freely (no strings).

If I am struck with awe at the beauty that religion has created, I can choose to respond to that. I need not deny the horror, the obscene squalor, of much religious history and behavior, but I need not let that deny me what is beautiful and good in the same tradition.

Whenever I find something that moves me and inspires me—it may be a painful and even terrible thing as well as a beautiful and good one—I can choose that thing and make it part of my life. I can find it growing—sharply clear and astonishing—between the solid structures of religion or political or commercial systems, in the cracks between credal statements.

I can choose such things, as they catch my eye the way a flower can, whether lovingly cultivated or growing wild in a hedge or among garbage. They may be things I've known and forgotten and rediscovered or rescued or new things I've only just encountered (but they may prove to have roots in older knowledge). These can be what I live by, finding the courage and compassion and hope I have to have in order to live at all.

The image of a flower is disturbing, however, because flowers don't last.

If you get it home quickly and place it in water, a flower you pick may last a day or so, but children who make wreaths and bouquets of flowers usually discard them at the end of their play, by which time the flowers are limp and sad, and grown-ups must soon discard even the most elaborate and expensive flower arrangements. So one essential fact about flowers and the wreaths we may weave from them is that they are ephemeral—picked, fashioned, used and discarded in a day. Yet you can make them again next day, and again and again. The children make wreaths and grow up, and make them too, as adults, and die, and others come, yet the flowers endure from age to age because they are chosen again and again, woven into new wreaths.

Flowers are fragile: a child's foot crushes them to a green slime, and wreaths are destroyed by one ill-tempered tug or even by the clumsiness of the maker. Yet wreaths of flowers continue while empires fall. They are more vulnerable than a sandcastle when the tide comes in yet in their continuity they outlast a Norman castle with walls twelve feet thick.

It is important to know that these gifts we choose are only as strong as our love for them, our wisdom in understanding. And part of the wisdom is knowing that all human perception is partial, inadequate, and changes as cultures change and as we ourselves change.

Continuity

$\mathcal{T}$o realize how the image of these fragile gifts can truly liberate, and allow real choices, we have to notice at once that as humans we long for belief that endures. We *need* continuity, and that is the paradox of the gifts we choose, and cannot hold onto however much we want to.

In the flux and uncertainty of our life—our private life, our cultural life, our planet's life—we want to feel there are some things that endure, that we can hold onto and trust, that continue through all changes. Human beings have always felt like this. As soon as they could build anything—from Stonehenge and the pyramids and the colossal ruined temples of Malta, through the radiant architecture of the Athenians and the vast, intricate temples of Asia, to the soaring mysteries of the medieval cathedrals of Europe—people have created structures that would bear witness to and worship their enduring divinities. People have often expressed their beliefs in stone, the most enduring building material, because their own sense of vulnerability was compensated by works of faith that were not vulnerable but that they believed would sustain the vision for themselves and their descendants forever, unchanging.

But in the end, the buildings fall. Weather and wildness reclaim neglected temples; tourists trample over holy places that are no longer holy, because the beliefs they enshrined have shifted, as the ground shifted under their vast weight, and cracks appeared and sometimes were repaired and sometimes not.

We want our beliefs to be permanent when we are not. We long for continuity. When a prophet or a great teacher proclaims a new doctrine, his or her followers want that doctrine not just to offer hope now but also to provide it for their children and grandchildren. Yet always some reject that newness just because it seems to undermine the continuity of more ancient faith.

The Buddha, Jesus, Muhammad, each carried and lived an ancient tradition but taught it as, and in, a way so new it was shocking. So did Luther, so did Gandhi. And Mary Baker Eddy and many others. And all of them, whether they meant to or not, both ensured a continuity and destroyed it. Then their followers made haste to build another secure castle of faith, incorporating stones from older ones. Or so they thought. But if they were indeed stones from the old building they were put together in ways that often contradicted the doctrines of the old. The rituals seemed the same but they, too, shifted because symbols changed significance.

Generation after generation, believers desire continuity, and fight change and kill each other because of it. But however they struggle, change comes, and the meanings shift and the language slides and the structure has to be tied together with steel ropes or anathemas, until some people see that it doesn't work and try to rescue what seems best of the old, and start the whole cycle over again.

Yet, I repeat, we do need continuity. Without it we can't make sense of our lives, our world. Without it we would be like a person who has lost her memory—who has no identity, no family, no home, no friends, no job, because even though these are all present, claiming connections, the connections mean nothing without memory. So we continue to want to build solid structures of belief to give meaning and continuity to our lives, something we can pass on to our children. When we can't, we grieve for a loss that is fundamental.

This book is written mainly for people with at least memories of something called Christianity, because that is the religion I partially grew up in and later chose. It is written out of the conviction that yes, we need continuity but we won't ever find it simply by building religious castles—of stone, of belief, of ritual. When we do that we may indeed preserve something beautiful, but too often it is at the cost of denying the truth that meanings change. And if we deny that truth, we tell those who see how the changes of culture and the challenge of catastrophe undermine the castle, that they must choose what is comfortable and beautiful over what is true.

How can we resolve the spiritual paradox of the human longing—need—for continuity and the impossibility of ensuring it?

Choices

To answer that question raised by the spiritual paradox of the longing for continuity and the impossibility of guaranteeing it, we have to look at the nature of the real continuity that is there, that we can count on. The real continuity, quite simply, is made up of the day-to-day choices of men and women. People make "acts of faith," as they used to be called. They choose to value and cherish certain things which seem to them to be clear, beautiful—mysterious perhaps but true to the reality they experience around them. Feeling and intellect assent to something, not because it is unarguable but because it fits a learned perception of how things are, and might be. It is a personal act but also a communal one; indeed it is usually made because it seems to be the communal experience. When a statement about how things really are appeals to the minds and hearts of a number of people, they help each other reinforce the truth of it. Belief in a god, for instance, in whatever form and language, seems to millions to make sense of the reality they know, and has done so for as far back as we have signs of human life on earth, yet this massive continuity of belief, even in all its variety, means that people every day have chosen to assent to that belief, and have helped reinforce it in others. It is true that in very closely knit or rigidly ruled societies it may be difficult to conceive of not believing: belief may seem to be the "of course" choice, but still, for whatever reason, the belief *is* a choice and must be constantly re-chosen, since the human mind is where the belief resides.

Perhaps it is difficult for us to take such an idea seriously because we tend to think of religious truth as something separate from ourselves, a kind of supernatural "thing" that just is *there* (if it *is* at all, that is) and which demands a response from us. Churches create this impression by formulating creeds; they do that, usefully, to help express and pass on and clarify beliefs, and the moral systems that are deemed to flow from the creeds and which are felt to be necessary in order to ensure that believers live according to true teaching. Yet the whole edifice of religion depends only and simply on choices: choices that are renewed, or not renewed, whenever a human mind turns to consider a particular belief. Even when huge social pressures demand belief, the continuity still resides in the willingness to say "yes." If this were not so, the means of persuasion (gentle ones or savage ones) which religions—from huge systems to small sects—employ would not be necessary. You don't set up heavy systems of moral and social persuasion amounting even to blackmail to prevent something which isn't likely to happen. People make choices, and controlling and directing those choices is what organized religion has to do, or so "it" believes—that is, those in authority believe, and they believe this because they are aware at some level that *choice* is the basis of faith.

Many books of spirituality have been written on the subject of religious doubt—how to avoid it or overcome it—because the existence of doubt is the proof that faith rests on choice, and that choices can waver and change.

The continuity of faith is a continuity of constant renewal, not of once-for-all, unchangeable commitment. We may want it to be unchangeable, make vows to make it so, but it can't be unchangeable, because *people* do change. In human relationships this need for constant renewal is obvious. For instance, the existence of marriage programs and counselors (official and otherwise) testifies to the awareness that choices, however solemn and sincere, are not fixed but require renewal all the time. A relationship is not something "out there" to which people are tied but is purely the result of daily choices. To contemplate a belief that is proposed to the mind and heart, and to find it fitting and real and attractive is, in the image I suggested, to pick a flower. And since beliefs don't come singly but are linked in marvelous systems of symbol, we pick other flowers and weave them together. We choose each flower, each gift that we perceive because its reality answers to a reality in ourselves—our private selves, but they are inseparable from the selves of our culture and history. We make our choices out of the materials of our culture and then perhaps of other cultures of which we learn and which in turn become part of the language of reality which is our own, but is shared with so many others.

That is the *only way* faith and religion continue, or ever have. Every day we are offered these gifts, and we choose every day, because without our ever-renewed choices, the gifts don't last. The only continuity is renewal.

It is true that the flower image is limited, but there is one thing about it that is important for our understanding of all gifts and choices:

If we look at a flower—especially a wildflower—as a present reality, we know it is the result of an enormously complex process, whose being is itself complex and unique, wonderfully adapted to its surroundings, its soil and climate. Its wonder is clear to us and we are able to choose, to reach out and accept the gift.

It is not so easy with beliefs. The distortions of belief in the past have often become part of the very way that religion is presented to us. We can't see it clearly, as we can see a flower. It takes, perhaps, the moment of grief, of memory, of poignant association to make us even want to reexamine what we may have ceased to experience as a gift but rather have come to feel as an encumbrance, or even a threat to our integrity. But we may be drawn to look again differently because of some moment in life when the consuming needs of survival—of career, family, self-development—give way a little and, in a kind of panic, there is a twinge of longing for something more. We may remember that some people—perhaps once ourselves or our parents or friends we meet— seemed to have discovered something else. So we may decide to look again at what we have rejected or simply neglected, and if we are lucky we can see something we didn't notice before, or perhaps rediscover something in the context of a different kind of belief or spirituality.

When I was a child of eight, my family spent a few months in Venice. My family weren't churchgoers and churches to them were for sightseeing. But when I went with them I didn't look at the architecture or the pictures but at the rows of little candles on metal stands, and at the old women who came in to light another candle, and then to sit, dump the heavy straw shopping basket and look at the statue of the Madonna lit from below by the glow of banked flames. There was no doctrinal description, no instruction about why they did this, but the sight remained an enduring and poignant memory that later said something about a quality of faith. In that experience, I picked a flower which I later wove together with others; it wasn't a matter of believing *anything* but of recognizing a gift that was offered and choosing to accept it. I was too young to analyze the experience then, but that is what happened.

Getting close to some aspect of spirituality does not necessarily mean unraveling its history to understand how creeds change and symbols shift in meaning, though that can be very liberating. It has more to do with recognizing a level of reality that is important, even if it can't be explained or if the available explanations don't make sense. You don't need to be a botanist to accept a flower, and you don't need to be a theologian or an historian to touch the essential quality of a truth that is somewhere in among religious experience. We don't have to get expert permission to be moved and illumined by the gift which is offered, though it matters, in time, to understand why something had obscured the reality for us.

Most teachers of religion want people to make clear statements about what they believe, but belief is a very peculiar process, and making statements is only a small part of it and can even serve to obscure the more important parts. The point is that we don't have to wait until we are clear about what we believe, or even *that* we believe. Perhaps one may feel an odd hunger in response to the soaring arches of a Gothic cathedral, or be stirred by the quality of faith in another person, or gripped by longing because of a poem or a Welsh hymn tune or candles. Differently, the experience of grief or the spectacle of human wickedness or human compassion can stir up a deep need to *know*, to change. If any of these stirs something in us that seems poignant and true and fills us for the time with obscure longing and grief, makes us feel suddenly vulnerable, or angry, or awed, then that is enough. The explicit connection of the experience to religious systems may be there at some level but it doesn't immediately matter. The gift is offered freely; there are no strings attached.

Community

The choices we make of things that give us life are very personal but they are not private. Spirituality, tradition, belief are all communal things. They cannot be "private," indeed to talk about private beliefs is nonsense, because every belief we have comes to us from other people. Political beliefs, beliefs about health or morality—all are acquired from other people, people we know (parents, teachers) or from books or TV shows, and we may accept these beliefs or modify them or reject them, but if we do the last two it is because someone or something else has caused us to question and rethink the beliefs we first acquired. Likewise, we pass on beliefs to others, casually or passionately, and so influence *their* beliefs. Ultimately, belief is a personal thing and a personal responsibility, but it is not and cannot be private, any more than, for instance, the skills of a cabinetmaker or a musician or a weaver or a plumber or a computer programmer are private. They are all personal and what each one does is a personal act, but the skills for doing it are learned from others, and they in turn from others, and have a history behind them. They are community skills, and the community extends to and includes those who appreciate the skill, and pay for it and ensure that it continues. If we cling to the illusion that spiritual truth is a private possession, we are ungrateful and untruthful to those who cherished and lived that truth and so made it available to us, even if their way of expressing it doesn't make sense to us or fit our present needs. Spiritual truth is a communal affair, whether we like it or not, and part of the joy of discovering it is discovering how it has been experienced and lived by others in the past and present.

Christianity, like all great religions, is explicitly a communal affair in its theology, but part of the damage that has been done to it, and to so many who have been disillusioned by it, has arisen from interpreting community as a matter of walls. Everyone inside the wall is part of the community, this kind of thinking says, everyone outside it isn't.

Conversely, one of the attractions of religion, for many people, is the existence of a supporting community. From church events and local celebrations to church-led movements (for instance, in aid of refugees or the homeless or for the cancellation of third-world debt), the existence of groups of people who do things together and care for each other and others is enormously attractive to people living in a fragmented, mostly urban society. Indeed it is the experience of encountering such a helping community, for instance, at a time of illness or crisis, that draws many to join a religious group. And this is another of those choices which, having been made, is then held to have involved a whole lot of other choices which maybe have not really been made. So, for many, the attraction of becoming part of the friendships and energy of a group doing obviously good things is tempered by the implicit demand that people who do these things together must also be part of a total religious system to which assent must be given.

Yet in reality we are free to choose the strength and the truth of a community without automatically choosing its total creed. This doesn't rule out *any* particular aspect of spiritual systems that we may, in time, come to understand, and appreciate, and choose. We have to remember that all the people saying creeds are themselves picking flowers for their wreaths, though they may not recognize it. We are free to choose gifts that other people also choose; they are not private, they are freely offered. They are nobody's (and no group's) private possession.

Choosing an insight is a level of commitment, and then we can allow the insight to link up with other, scarcely seen, realities and soon, in some way or other, we experience the fact of community, seen or unseen.

Some people just like to sit in cathedrals. The soaring arches, the light through stained glass, the statues—even those damaged by long-ago

bigots—are statements about the people who made all this, their attitudes, their aspirations, and their failures. Just to sit and look at all this is
to experience a community. To recognize this unseen community is an
important spiritual choice, for it links us not only to the makers but to
others who come here, come searching for something or celebrating
something or just wanting a place to be quiet, or escape, or weep.

Many people are inspired by a forest, with its intimation of the
community of so many lives—plants, insects, animal and human. Or a
movie or a picture gallery can offer amazing revelations of gifts to be
chosen. These are personal experiences, yet the gifts they offer us are gifts
of community, of shared vision, courage, beauty, hope.

Nobody's choices are exactly like those of others, or even exactly like their own previous choices. Choices change, as people grow and
learn; yet, as we've seen, the choices have a continuity, and the continuity gives a power to the choices to draw from the person, and through
each person, the community that is there even when unseen.

When I was in my early teens I was immensely attracted by religion. In a family that had few religious beliefs and didn't talk about
them, I couldn't talk about this attraction; instead, I picked flowers—
though of course I didn't think of it like that. I read lives of saints, I
looked at statues in churches, I cherished a tiny glass rosary of whose use

I had no idea. But somewhere in all that, I was sure, I was in touch with people who shared a mystery that I needed to understand. Somewhere, I knew, there was the community I longed for.

So making a choice to take some moment of spiritual awareness and choose to be grateful, to value it, to rejoice in it, is also to enter the vast company of those who search for truth. This sense of being part of something large and yet intimate, seen or unseen, explicit or quite vague—or even just wanting to be part of it—is a true and deeply important insight.

The importance of this awareness can't be overstated, because it corresponds to the nature of human being, which is interdependent down to the last molecule, whether we like it or not. To make deliberately even one choice of spiritual truth draws us into a great—perhaps the greatest—common earthly undertaking. It is a challenge, but also a huge satisfaction and comfort. The comfort, the sense of solidarity, is needed, because such choices make up a discipline that requires ever renewed and deliberate decision. The sense of being part of something beyond oneself—simply the knowledge that other people haven't given up—can make a difference.

Living Free

Spiritual truth is not only about moments of discovery, a sudden feeling of illumination. To make sense of life you need sense, not just feeling. Those moments when something new breaks in are important, but it is what lies beyond them that matters, what you come to see through the door that has opened. It is a matter of choice—and a choice is conscious and deliberate; feeling may present us with a choice but it doesn't choose for us. To choose is to add an element to your life, and it is a choice even if it is something you learned in childhood, or accepted without understanding much about it.

To discover more, to discover further implications that flow from that moment means a series of choices: trying to understand, meditating, practicing, reading, learning. At each step you can decide it's too difficult, boring, silly, too hung about with ancient phrases or repulsive ideologies. Having chosen yesterday doesn't let you off choosing today, but you also don't have to choose today. How do you distinguish the quality that attracted you from the inevitable historical flotsam that the stream of a religion accumulates?

It helps to realize that a system of faith—a personal one or a whole religious one—is a view of reality, but it is important to know that it only exists because of choices made by people, and constantly renewed by people. There is neither the need nor even the possibility of holding every aspect of any religious system in the consciousness of each adherent at every moment. Even the most rigidly orthodox of believers can't do it. They may recite a creed, enumerating statements of belief, but at any given moment these can never be totally grasped and those that are, not wholly. Some are in the forefront of the mind, others are background, perhaps to be considered another time, perhaps just taken for granted and not much thought about. A person looking at a meadow of wildflowers may choose to pick some but know that others are still there—though the image is unlikely to appeal to people who perceive religion as a castle of closely fitted masonry. Things that get expressed as articles of belief are a complex of event, thought, symbol, history, ritual, celebration, developed and finally crystallized after all of it has been mixed and added to and subtracted from, often through many generations. These complex creations may be artificially parceled out as articles of creeds, but they are actually found in cultural company with all kinds of opinions, symbols, customs, prejudices. Some of these articles of belief eventually cease to make the spiritual connections that create a living whole.

If once we can recognize the complexity and interconnectedness of spiritual truth, and how impossible it is to encapsulate it in categories and forms (however useful and even necessary these may be in some respects), we also come upon the liberating fact that the package deal we are offered in much religion is more about keeping people in order than about sharing truth.

So if the bargain, on the whole, turns out to be a poor one, then what is valuable is often refused along with what seems shoddy. It needs to be said that such an impression may be a wrong one—what at one stage of life seems to us foolish or deceptive may turn out in the end to be as worthwhile as what was first desired, perhaps obscured by false language, but that is another step and another time, and meanwhile it seems a pity to let go of a perception of truth because it appears to come attached to something we don't want. The choice is made now, in the face of this awareness of truth. We are offered a gift in all its mystery and liveliness and fragility, and stand in awe of it, and with wonder we perceive how it is connected to other gifts which we have chosen because each reverberates at the heart of ourselves. Each is poignantly vulnerable, but it gives life, here and now. Tomorrow we will be offered another like it and choose it and perhaps add others, aware always that continuity depends on the courage of our common choices, and nothing else.

A Wreath of My Own

I began writing this book out of a moment of insight that I needed to pursue—but I really didn't know where it would take me. The image of paradoxical fragility, strength and continuity kept unfolding. It opened up new questions, and as I tried to answer them I discovered more. It was a moving and exciting experience, and a liberating one. Yet although the work began as a means to discover a way through for myself, it soon unfolded into a desire to share what I was discovering with others who have shared the experience of disillusion, betrayal, sadness and longing. So the rest of this book is simply a description of the choices I made, and I have described them in the hope that they will inspire others to realize the possibility and the urgency of not losing heart, and of making truthful and life-giving choices whenever we are offered them.

What follows, then, are my own particular choices, making up my "wreath" of chosen flowers, at this particular point in my life. Many years ago the wreath would have been different. Even a few years ago it would have been different. And a few years from now it may be different again. Yet there is a continuity that fills me with delight, even awe, at the discoveries that keep on happening. As I set out to write down my own chosen gifts, I know I shall discover more as I write. There is no particular order, though some connections are clear enough.

This part of the book is not a "creed." It is a description of a few choices of the heart, discoveries that make sense to me, though I know how much in each there is still to discover, and how many more there are out there that I will never choose because my mind and heart, as well as my time, are limited. But perhaps some of them will inspire someone else to look further and discover a gift they need.

Many of these flowers that I chose are indeed rescued, with gratitude, from the religion I learned to love, sometimes rediscovering something I had set aside because the way I was taught it seemed, eventually, unreal and distorted. Others may not seem to be "religious" at all, but I think they are spiritual and that is important because one of the mistakes made by some religions is to draw a line between what is religious and what isn't. Because of this, at this point I think I have to add a warning. It is that what follows is not, as I said, a "creed" but it naturally includes things that are the rough stuff out of which creeds are, or might be, made. So it may seem startling, even shocking, that the "flowers" in my wreath do not necessarily include elements that believers of various kinds may consider essential. But I am simply saying what it is that inspires, draws me, for my life now. I am not saying that other aspects of those spiritual truths I am trying to express are negligible, but only that I, like all seekers, am still seeking, discovering, uncovering. Indeed the very process of writing this has been an astonishing experience of discovery, which is why I hope other people will want to identify the flowers from which their own wreaths are made, and be grateful for them and amazed and delighted. They may, as I have done, find in this discovery the strength to go on knowing and living their truth in a world saturated with sorrow and evil. Every truthful choice we make and reflect on and live from is a point of new possibility for good. Every time we choose, with gratitude, we bring new hope into the world.

PART II

Chosen Gifts

Interdependence

$\mathcal{A}$ few years ago, in the middle of a rather dull religious conference, it suddenly struck me that the Christian doctrine of the Trinity was actually a good description of reality as modern physics and biology have increasingly revealed it. The nature of all reality is interdependence. Everything that is, is linked ultimately to every other thing; everything that happens affects every other happening, so that, to use a much quoted example, the flutter of a butterfly's wing in Australia may end as a hurricane in Florida.

In a way, we've always known this—the chain of consequences is part of daily experience. The farmer knows how the weather and the soil affect the crops and animals and so his own future, though he or she may not know the complex causes of weather patterns. The financier knows how the vagaries of the market spell prosperity or ruin for many and can trace some of them to events such as changes of government, though much is unexplained. The connections are dauntingly complex, the chains of consequences are long and much more far-reaching than we often want to recognize. The web of good and of evil consequences that seems to originate in one act of generosity or of hate is the unpredictable stuff of our lives as individuals, families, nations. What unknown complexities of changed imagination led to the moment when the Berlin wall began to go down? And how much, both good and evil, flowed from that moment that no one expected or could control? There are moments of decision we can perceive, in hindsight, as fateful, yet each was the result of a million other decisions, our own and other people's. And the web is not, of course, just human—we interconnect and our lives are changed by geography and climate, by natural resources or the lack of them, by other creatures (including bacteria!). At every moment we experience ourselves as made out of a never-ceasing network of exchange, beautiful and terrifying.

Poets have celebrated the interconnectedness of reality, mystics have been filled with awe by it, superstitions try to catch it, all science is based on it, modern physics has traced and mapped some of it, and scientists exploring the wonder of subatomic reality have themselves been driven to use mystical language to express the quality of interdependence they perceive.

This interdependence is also in movement, it is dynamic, it never stops. There is a constant flow of exchange of life and being at every level. Not only do *things* change all the time (the crystals in the rocks of mountains change, though not as fast as soil structure and plant development and the economy), but because of this the relationships, the exchange of being between things, change at every moment. Evolution of species is only one, fairly slow, example of the never-ending movement of the dance of exchanged life in creation.

As soon as we say "creation" we have to say "create." Where does all this come from? How did reality get this way? In the terms of any kind of theology, of any religion, creation must be *made out of* the creator. What else could it be made of? If creation is an infinite exchange of being and life, from the grains of earth's dust to the farthest nebulae, then it must be because that is the nature of the divine stuff of which it is made, which it expresses, of which it is the image.

An interdependent divinity? A divinity of exchanged life? A divinity within which life is poured out and received, and given back, without limit or reserve? This seems to be a good definition of love. If believers want to say that God is love, then they are saying that the reality of God is life given and received. But it is not self-sufficient, enclosed; the nature of such an exchange is to have no limits, by its very nature to be poured out without end. What we call creation, then, cannot be an extra, it must be of the essence of the kind of divinity we struggle to name when we say "trinity": clumsy though the thought may be yet it does say that divinity is not a single, self-sufficient, "outside" power but something that requires new, strange words to express even a hint of its nature, which is our nature.

We must also say that if it is love, if it is exchange, if it has no limits, then this divinity, this ultimate reality, is passionate, it is fertile, it is vulnerable, it is necessarily *eccentric*, it is wild and inexplicable and unpredictable yet faithful (because it has by definition no capacity for deception) and above all compassionate, because there is no "place" in such a reality for exclusion.

But also, this impossibility of separateness means that whatever we mean by God or Goddess is also our own most essential nature, it is what makes us and what joins us in the exchanges of being. Which makes it all the stranger that the kinds of exchanges of being that humans deliberately set up are often so destructive and cruel. That is a fact of which someone seeking to choose an offered gift must be aware.

At the same time, I suppose if my wreath were broken up and I could only have one flower, this is the one I would have to keep choosing. I believe in divinity whose nature can at least be hinted at by using the symbol of trinity, one found in ancient cultures long before it was discovered by Christians as a way of imagining the unimaginable.

Sin

*I*f I say, "interdependence," and experience it consciously, I am awed by it and comforted by it and yet also I am afraid of it. I am right to fear it because the ever-moving web of changing reality is woven of evil as well as good, and they are so closely interwoven that we cannot separate them. "Sin" is not something one would, at first sight, choose to pick as a source of inspiration and courage, yet it seems I must be willing to acknowledge evil as intrinsic to reality, not something that can be separated and discarded.

Many kinds of spirituality have labored to do that. We have made lists of sins and labored to overcome them, punished ourselves and dwelt in guilt because this Augean stable can never, ever be swept out. Too many Christians have tried to eliminate it by locating it in material reality, especially human bodies (and *especially* female bodies) and so tried to avoid sin by ignoring or persecuting bodies and despising the beauty of creation. The results of all this have been crippling to the spirit, and ineffective. "Sin" is still there, more obsessing than ever. Somehow I have to choose to know the reality of evil interconnected with good, and live with it.

Perhaps that means understanding that what we call "sin" is really somehow a failure to experience and respond to interdependence. This can be deliberate. I can want to claim exemption from the effects of circumstances I don't like. I don't want, for instance, to be hurt by someone's dislike, so I think of reasons to avoid that person, thinking that will stop me from getting hurt. It doesn't work, because instead I am caught in another web of pretense and anxiety.

In a far more drastic and far-reaching way, prosperous Western nations have allowed themselves to believe they can have—and have a right to—exemptions from evils that affect other cultures. We have tried to believe we could eliminate diseases and want and be forever prosperous. If our level of security and comfort was to be obtained by exploiting the labor of others, or polluting our earth and water, we managed not to think too hard about that. Categorizing some nations or races or particular categories of people as enemies helped us exclude them rather than recognize interdependence with them. When fear and uncertainty are forced on us, the first thing we want to do is find the sinners and eliminate them.

In small and big ways, then, I am called on not just to recognize but to experience interdependence, and it is uncomfortable to say the least. I am called to respond to that awareness, with my heart and my time, my space, my money—I am not my own. If I refuse to recognize who and what I am, it is the denial of reality, which is the exchange of life. The denial diminishes me, imprisons me. That is sin. If the denial continues, deliberately and permanently, that is, perhaps, hell.

My response to the pain of interdependence has to be real—but part of my response is the recognition that I am not able to do very much about it. I can't put everything right, I am limited. However generous or powerful I am, what I can do to mitigate suffering or confront evil is not much, in the scale of things, and that knowledge of limitation hurts. The hurt is the effect of *sin*—the pain in some instance of not being able fully to experience the giving and receiving of life. But this is the condition of our lives—whether we try to opt out of the exchanges deliberately, by refusing to give, or whether giving is constrained simply by how things are (our nature, our situation). That is sin—not just personal wrong choices but also existence in a system swayed by greed and fear.

So, to me, sin is not so much something people do but just the pain of not being able, in our human condition, fully to experience the giving and receiving of life. Because of fear we can and do *choose* to refuse that exchange, and can go to unimaginably horrible lengths to resist it, to allocate blame for what we fear and act on that blame. That fear results in racism, in genocide. It fills the prisons and divides families and nations. It gives corrupt politicians and corporations and terrorists power, because they appeal to that fear. To dwell for a moment on a global situation that affects everyone, this fear has created a situation in which the United States, and other nations that act with it, respond to the despair that fosters terrorism by spending billions on weapons and surveillance in attempts to crush the elusive enemy.

After the horror of the destruction of New York's twin towers with the loss of thousands, there was deep grief but it was also a blow to the nation's sense of invulnerability. This kind of thing happened to other places—London, Ireland, Cambodia, Rwanda—not to the mighty U.S.A. The reaction was huge anger and fear, and then the nation was offered a way to deal with the anger and the fear by locating an enemy and setting out to destroy it. Like most such responses to fear, this was a denial of the reality of interdependence. The denial is a denial of reality, so actions that spring from it are based in fantasy because of the refusal to dare to experience the truth of national as well as personal and cosmic interdependence. This denial is hugely expensive and gains nothing but more terror, yet if a fraction of that cost were donated to desperately poor nations to help them build schools and roads and hospitals and a local economy, the effect before long would be to drain away the support for terrorism among people who now support it because of their bitterness and hopelessness, even if they take no active role. This is the insanity of the conspirators of fear and greed. This is what sin is like.

We all experience that monstrous fear in some measure, and so also share some measure of sin, because the web of exchanged life is made up of happiness and sorrow, gain and loss, health and disease, prosperity and want. We want the good things and are afraid of the bad ones. To live in the exchange of life is not to pretend it's all comfortable, or can be, but to *choose* to be what we, in any case, are—interdependent. That gives us a chance to let ourselves understand the nature of the evil which is done in our name, not in order to burden ourselves with guilt but to free ourselves to make the choices that are within our reach, soberly and with compassion. How we use our money and our votes, how we speak, in public and private, how we bear witness to truth as we know it—these are decisions we can make. These are ways to mitigate the suffering, share hope, go on giving. We won't ever know or give fully—we really *are* sinful people. But we can learn to understand and so be at peace with what we are.

Compassion

*T*hinking of the choice to know and love interdependence led inevitably to confronting the pain of that interdependence, and the sin that is the result of refusing to live the exchanges. And what makes it possible to bear the hurt that is inherent in the exchange of life, and to overcome the fear, is compassion. But compassion is not just a human emotion. If it can truly liberate from fear, if in a sense it makes possible the exchange of life, then surely the nature of reality is compassion, for compassion is the giving and receiving of life without condition and in spite of all hurt. Yes, truly, the nature of reality is love, and that's what I am talking about, and yet I find I need the word "compassion" more, at least for now.

As I write this I find myself discovering more about interdependence, and about sin. These realities are not separate, yet the thoughts unfold in different ways, like waves that fan out onto the beach, and the foaming crescents from different directions meet each other, and overlap and flow together, and then are drawn back into the sea, to gather and flow landwards again and again. Can such fragile things be for me a sign of such huge realities? I think so, because my mind is limited. I can only choose a little reality at a time, and reflect on it and cherish it.

So, now, I want to use the word "compassion" because in some ways it is more precise than "love." "Love" can express and include desire, neediness, passion, jealousy, possessiveness and more, but compassion by its nature is not exclusive, can never be possessive. The sense of the word is "suffering with," but the Latin word we translate as "suffering" is not only about pain, it is about undergoing any kind of experience. Indeed, in English even the word "suffering" was once used to mean "allow," as in "suffer the children to come to me." So compassion means the will, the intent, to share experience, good or bad, and not to be deterred from doing so. But we mostly think of compassion as entering into bad experience, because the bad times are those when an unlimited, generous sharing is most needed. The inevitably painful nature of living means that compassion is what can keep us faithful to the reality of exchanged life, not rejecting it because it hurts.

There is a midrash told about the biblical story in the book of

Exodus when the people of Israel were being led to freedom through the parted waters of the Red Sea and the chariots of Pharaoh, chasing after them, were drowned in the returning waters. In this midrash the angels, who were all ready to begin a celebration of the great liberation, found The Holy One weeping. They were naturally very surprised, and asked the reason. The Holy One replied, "Are not these Egyptians also my children? And should I not weep for them?" This is a startling description of compassion, because compassion cannot be partisan, or choose to weep for the death of one and not another.

Yet how can the nature of reality be compassionate when the whole earth, in every part and through all its history, is impregnated through and through with destruction, with suffering and the infliction of suffering by all kinds of beings, by the suffering of the earth itself and, in the case of humans, by the deeper evil of hate and deliberate cruelty—the sin I've been talking about? But we are not talking about a God who *is* compassionate, an exterior God *being* compassionate, but about compassion as the nature of God and the nature of reality. And if that reality is interdependence, which means the endless flow of change and exchange of being, that *involves* destruction: the death of stars, or of whole ecosystems, as vast climatic and geological shifts occur, as well as the "smaller" deaths (but what does "small" mean here?) of trees and humans and butterflies. And newness arises from these deaths, indeed without death newness would be impossible. Change means suffering, death and new beginnings. Humans suffer and in turn cause suffering, often through fear and ignorance. They devise ways of thinking to protect themselves from fear and to justify destruction and killing. A compassionate God might grieve for all this, untouched, but a divinity whose *nature* is the exchange of life both gives life and receives life in this process. Such a divinity is not just touched by the exchange, but the exchange is deep within it and through it, so that every event of good or evil, beauty or horror, is part of that exchange which is reality. Compassion, then, is inherent; it is the very breath of the cosmos, of creation. That is why evil is not the last word, although destruction, pain and fear are real and inevitable.

We, as conscious beings, can make choices. We cannot choose not to feel pain, because pain is the nature of a changing universe, but we can choose how we respond. We can respond consciously from the deepest part of ourselves, which is the deepest reality, which is compassion, and so we can set in motion another chain of cause and effect, one which shifts the direction of the cosmos by liberating in it a little more of the power of compassion which is its true nature.

This is a flower I have quite recently picked for my wreath. I had not realized that compassion is not just human but cosmic. It makes the world feel different.

Prayer

*T*here is one kind of response to the pain of life which seems naturally to need to be chosen, to become part of how we live interdependence, and that is prayer.

When people say "prayer," they mostly mean asking God for something. There are other kinds of prayer but that is the one people either believe in strongly, even desperately, or can't accept at all, and it is one I am concerned with here because it has to do with compassion, and sin. One reason for not believing in prayer is simply that it requires an interference: God (or something) interrupts the normal chain of cause and effect and makes things come out differently. And that is what people who pray hope will happen—that a sick person will heal, peace will come to a war-torn land, money to pay off a debt will turn up, a job will be obtained, rain will come on the parched land. Does God interfere on behalf of those who pray hard enough? Does it *work*?

Clearly, not always, and that's why some get turned off the whole idea. The loved and prayed-for child dies just the same. The family that prayed for months loses their house anyway. The war and the famine drag on. Yet some hospital studies have shown that patients who were prayed for recovered more often and better than patients with comparable problems who were not prayed for. It isn't surprising that one doctor commented, "Even if it's true I won't believe it," because the idea of prayer being "effective" cuts across what has come to be regarded as scientific, as science has been defined in the last two hundred years.

It was because of thinking about interdependence, the wonderful exchanges of being which are all reality, that it dawned on me that prayer wasn't about interference but about an act which is, like all acts, the end result of countless causes and the cause of innumerable effects.

Every moment is like that. An unimaginably complex and huge sequence of events led to this one, present, unique moment. To pray is an act, and the person who acts in this way does so as a response to that sequence. The past of a person who prays contains experiences and ideas that make him or her choose to pray, perhaps for the thousandth time, perhaps for the first time. And because prayer is an act, like any other act it changes everything that comes after it, not just or necessarily in the way envisaged by the person praying but in all kinds of ways that aren't, and never will be, known.

What kinds of changes? It's one thing to say that prayer is an act, and therefore must have an effect, but how does it work? We might call it a "movement of spirit," which after all means breath. To call it "energy" also helps because we feel comfortable talking about energy, and we have even got used to thinking of hospitals using meditation as a treatment for cancer. There is so much we don't know about the exchanges of energy and matter. (At this point in history we are less inclined to laugh at people who talk to plants or play Mozart to cows.)

For me, the revelation was understanding that you *can't* interfere—nor does God. Prayer, or the answer to prayer, is not "interference," it's an act in the wonderful web of cause and effect, and everything that follows, in all directions, is other than it would have been without that act. If I accept that the energy, the spiritual power, of prayer is a reality, then prayer matters, is powerful, in ways we don't understand and can't predict. It could, if there were enough of it, end wars, as minds are changed. Can it change the weather? How do we know? (We do know that if we chose to change our habits of pollution we might reverse global warming.)

So we can say "It is karma," or "God's will be done," or "please, please!" and any of these make sense, because God's will is another word for the nature of reality, that web of interdependence which is creator and creation. So I just have to accept in amazement that at this unique point of intersection of past and future I can choose to act in a way which will release a power of goodness into all the exchanges of being that flow out from this moment. It may be only a very small "power of goodness"—but how do we know? Can we measure the power of prayer by the worthiness of the one who prays? Since no prayer (no act) is isolated, but all are part of the web of life, who knows how powerful even my prayer might be, as it flows in the rivers of the spirit?

All this is a different way of thinking. It carries with it a strange sense of responsibility as well as opportunity. Above all prayer suddenly seems such a *natural* thing to do, because it simply *is* part of how things happen.

Food

*I*t seems like a bump from the sublime to the—well, not ridiculous but—ordinary. From prayer to food. But they are quite closely connected, as all the prayers before, after—and for—food show. It is ordinary—but also extraordinary.

I believe in food. Food is not just any old stuff you put in your stomach, though for those who are desperately hungry anything edible is food. But to reduce human beings to such a state is already to desecrate their humanity, to deprive them of the power actually to use food in a meaningful way. "We are what we eat," and this isn't just about good physical nutrition, it is about how the way we use, or misuse, food shapes our minds and hearts, and teaches us about our relationship to other things and people. The now famous President, referring to what children should have for school dinners, who thought ketchup should "count" as a vegetable, had long ago lost touch with the reality of food as a sharing of life, as pleasure, as cause for gratitude, as celebration, as deserving of respect and even awe. (This is not to say that ketchup isn't an excellent form of food, when well made, though often it isn't.)

It has taken a long time for the human race to develop (if that is the word) to the point where it can routinely treat food as mainly a commodity (you make lots of money out of it) or a problem (it can make you fat or ill). Both attitudes, of course, have a long history, but you have only to walk through a supermarket or watch TV commercials to perceive that food-as-profit and food-as-problem take up huge amounts of the attention we pay to food.

A wonderful and ironic thing has happened: the very drive of huge corporations to ensure that food becomes *only* a commodity has driven millions of ordinary people into revolt. People are asking for food that is not drenched in chemicals from field to shelf. People are refusing to eat food genetically modified in order to ensure a monopoly of production and sale by a few vast chemical and agribusiness corporations. If they can afford it, more people are willing to pay a bit more to buy food that is grown in healthy soil or from animals raised in healthy conditions and not injected with drugs. They are even realizing that this food only costs more because governments subsidize the farmers who use chemicals or genetically modified seed (or both) and do so because the chemical and biotech and agribusiness companies subsidize the politicians. They are realizing that when we buy "cheap" food we are buying food kept cheap not only by subsidies but because the farmers aren't asked to pay the real cost of the kind of agriculture they are taught; for instance, the cost of the contamination of water supplies: we pay with our taxes to clean that up. The destruction of fish and other life in rivers and estuaries, of birds and other wild creatures, the degradation of the soil itself— all these are among the real costs of "cheap" food. Better information and the growing distrust of chemically grown, altered, treated, colored, flavored and preserved food are showing more people that food is not, of itself, a problem.

Another wonderful thing is happening—though not nearly fast enough. The concern about food, the scares about contamination, the awareness of routine use of toxic chemicals at every stage from field to table, have also made more people in the wealthy West aware that not only are those who produce the food even more exposed to health risks than the consumer but that the cost of cheap food is often the devastation of rural economies in the third world and the seizing of land from small farmers for big agribusiness. This grim information is drawing more people to realize the reality of our interdependent world in one very acute way. We eat from each other's lives, literally. But that can be changed from a deathly truth to a life-giving one if it leads to changes in the way we use food—trade it, buy it, meditate on it, legislate about it, cook it, eat it. So the problem is seen to be, not food, but how we use it, not just as a commodity (though of course we need to sell and buy it) but as a gift that binds the world together.

In Christianity, Eucharist, the Lord's supper, is about gifts of food through which divine life is received. The ritual celebrates, at a very intense level, the fact that divine life (compassionate, interdependent) is shared in every loaf of (real!) bread, every carefully cooked meal, every skillfully made bottle of wine.

All religions have celebrated the great holy days with special meals. On a TV program celebrating Hanukkah a speaker quoted a saying that summed up all Jewish celebrations: "They tried to kill us, they couldn't—let's eat!" To celebrate the great salvations, the seasons of the year from planting to harvesting, the seasons of human life (birth, marriage, death) people eat and drink the best food and wine they can provide, and special foods belong to each celebration in each tradition. Families and communities have their own traditional celebrations. Special recipes are handed down from generation to generation.

At certain times, also, almost all religions and spiritual traditions require believers to abstain from food, to fast, and certain people in many traditions choose to abstain for long periods from all but the simplest food. This is not a rejection of food but an affirmation that food is a gift, and that to do without it for a while can make us better able to accept it as holy and not abuse it, or allow others to be abused so that we may eat. At the very least this seems to be about calling people to know that food is a gift and not to be taken for granted. Without food, we die. We owe to food a certain awe. It is about being alive—or not. I am doubtful about cookbooks whose recipes consist of combining readymade foods—cans of this, packets of that—in the name of speed and simplicity. I am glad if overworked people who think of cooking as too difficult for them are thereby encouraged to try it, but I hope they can somehow discover that sense of being connected to old and new skills of growing and sharing and enhancing food that comes from handling fresh stuff, and feeling all the grandmothers before us, and their love and their overcoming of shortages, their ways of making the most of not much and being inspired and satisfied. I came across a lovely poem celebrating women making apple pies:

> "My mother said her mother could weigh flour
> in her hands and measure vinegar with her eyes
> Her mother rolled crust with a rolling pin
> cut by her father from a single apple limb.
> My mother cut stars to eat from what remained . . .
> My God, think of it, all those women

on fine September afternoons like these,
bent against an angle of light and rolling pie crust,
not worrying
seeing things whole."

On the other hand there is a kind of snobbish tyranny fostered by TV programs which demands that people produce exquisite and varied meals every day. Does *every* meal have to be a banquet? If we could re-learn to enjoy very good, simple things—bread, fruit, eggs from hens that enjoy life (which actually can provide really "fast" food)—we might also enjoy the big celebrations more and the occasional "gourmet" meals.

Food comes from the earth and is only as healthy as the earth, and the earth is only as healthy as we allow it to be. It is good to experience this connection, if only in a window box of herbs and the odd tomato plant. Putting in seeds or seedlings, watching them grow, finding ways to deal with pests, watering, harvesting—it's work that is all about interdependence and divinity and compassion: compassion because people who grow things (as opposed to people who run factory-farms) feel *with* the things they grow, whether they raise chickens, cows, cabbages or a child's patch of mustard-and-cress. They care and worry and mourn and rejoice. And then they celebrate.

One more thing—and it is at the heart of food. Everyone may

sometimes very much enjoy a solitary meal (perhaps with a book in the sun, or by the fire) but food is essentially about community. Growing food is a communal activity. Even for a lone gardener. Someone else grew the seed or the seedlings, gave advice (in a gardening book?), supplied tools or seaweed fertilizer or canes, or jars to hold the resultant jam or jelly. The soil is the result of eons of geology and has probably been dug by many others before. Unless one lives on a desert island, others will share what has been grown. Even the hermit learned from someone else how to grow things.

I believe in food—and it would be good to think that one day everyone will enjoy food that is good for them, and enough of it. But food is magic, and children eating stuff with little real goodness in it can, by their pleasure, miraculously transform it into food, and it will do them good, and it will be a true experience of divine interdependence.

Christmas

*T*his wreath really is a careful weaving, a created thing far more meaningful than its parts. One discovery, one gift chosen, brings one to contemplate another with new curiosity and care, and then to make a new choice to add to it, the new whole being more wonderful and strange than its parts.

It is not hard to see the connection between food and Christmas. This is a winter festival of northern Europe, which has spread to America and even to Australia where immigrants brought it and where people sweat over the roast turkey. It spread to warmer European and other countries for commercial reasons. Once, the southern European Christian winter festival was Epiphany, and indeed that date persisted into the Middle Ages in the north too. "The Cherry Tree carol"

GIFTS IN THE RUINS

has the unborn Jesus announce, "On the sixth day of January my birthday shall be," and the feast of the Three Wise Men who brought gifts to the Christ child was a good day to give gifts. Then for the Danes and Dutch the feast of St. Nicholas (Santa Klaus) on December 6th was a day for giving, because of St. Nicholas who secretly gave dowries to young girls faced with slavery—really meaning prostitution—for lack of a dower. As for Father Christmas, he was a curious Victorian growth, with echoes, perhaps, of the ancient pagan "Green Man" whose leafy face gazes out from medieval church carvings, and of the medieval "Lord of Misrule" whose jolly license it was to lead the merry-making for those twelve days without too much regard for propriety. Somehow he got mixed up with Santa Klaus and acquired a red coat and a beard and became attached to the feast of the Nativity of Christ, and ripe for exploitation by manufacturers of toys and other gifts, from the shoddy to the super-expensive.

It is easy to hate the Christmas that has emerged from all this, a time of anxiety and tired children and debt and bad temper and too many parties and too much drink. Sometimes I wish I could wipe it off like an out-of-date diagram on a blackboard and start again.

Yet at the heart of Christmas is the coincidence of two totally different things which are both wonderful. One is its northern origins. Christmas is the Christianized successor to winter festivals that were held at the solstice, the longest night of the year, the heart of the winter cold and darkness which, in northern latitudes, engulfed everyone for long months.

As people tried to keep warm in the halls and cottages, with logs and turves, lighted by rushes dipped in tallow or, if they were richer, with candles, they worried about whether the fuel would hold out, whether there was enough grain stored or meat salted to keep them alive until the new growth. Good King Wenceslas looked out to notice a man picking up sticks because he needed them to keep him and his family alive. The king knew the man was in dire need and the point of the story is that he did something about it, unlike most kings. To run out of fuel, or stored food, was to die.

Yet in that climate and in the face of that fear people got together and held huge celebrations. As the light vanished earlier and earlier each day they gambled on the sun's good will not to abandon them, in effect saying, "We trust you," but keeping their fingers crossed, and used great quantities of food, burning the great Yule log (sharing the life the sun provided for them in the tree from the years before) as a prayer that he would not let them down in the year to come. It seems crazy, with the worst of the cold months still ahead, to spend precious stores, yet there is in this a deep sanity, a trust in the goodness of things, a defiance of death, a willingness to outface cold and fear with the warmth of rejoicing. The little lights of Christmas trees and windows, the lighted shops, the flaming Christmas pudding, are faint memories of those older and courageous rituals, but as they shine in the midwinter darkness they too lift the heart, promising the return of the light. We have different reasons for fear, most of them unconnected to the seasons, but still that attitude of combined defiance, trust and celebration is potent.

If it is an accident of climate and dates that Christians celebrate the birth of Christ on a day close to that of the winter solstice, it is a happy one. The Romans had a holiday—a rather wild one—at that time of year, and the church attached the feast of the Nativity to it, either to sanctify it, or distract from its pagan nature, or both—who knows? It wasn't an important feast for a long time, but there is a human appeal about this celebration that gradually embedded it in popular religion, eventually with the help of St. Francis, who is reputed to have created the first Christmas crib, with real cattle and a model baby Jesus. Somehow, anyway, that became a tradition, and even horrible plaster statues have not succeeded in effacing the power of this vision of divine compassion lying in a cattle trough.

Most likely Jesus wasn't born on December 25. Maybe he wasn't born in Bethlehem. Some scholars (more the media, really) find a strange delight in trying to prove to the credulous that they have been conned, but the doubters may well be correct. The stable, the star, the shepherds, the humble couple, their threatened baby—these are stories for peasants and children. Well, we are learning the hard way that peasants often understand the ways of the earth and its plants better than researchers employed by multinational corporations. Our culture operates by singularly narrow and ultimately unscholarly categories in which something is *either* myth *or* historical. What we are, perhaps, painfully learning is that our grownup ways of understanding reality are limited by the ways we have been taught to think. There is a lot we don't know, and it may be that the best way to learn more is to explore both myth and history with humility and awe. The child in the manger tells us something about compassion, about the nature of all babies, including that one: those terrifyingly vulnerable bearers of love and hope and our future.

Babies

*C*hristmas and babies easily go together, and I believe in babies.
A few years ago the wonderful mystery writer P. D. James took
a detour from detection and wrote a strange book called *Children of Men*.
It is about not being able to have children—not just some infertile couple, but a fate falling upon the whole human race for some reason never
spelled out. So it describes a society struggling to cope with the fact that
there will be no more babies to grow up and take on the human task.

The novel explores the measures taken by a government faced
with the need to encourage the swift departure of elderly whom no one
can afford to support and to keep a population with no future beyond
itself somehow contented and entertained. In such a situation, the book

suggests, a creeping despair mists the nation, blights all the normal human pursuits of study, work, planning. What do you strive for, work for, plan for, if there is no one to carry it all into the future? One might suppose that those who never wanted children anyway would be less affected, but as we read we know that this unnamed doom has sucked the heart out of all life, leaving only cynicism, stoic endurance, unbridled pleasure-seeking that brings no pleasure, and outbreaks of ritual violence.

The plot takes an extraordinary twist at the end, linked to the author's long-evident fascination with religion and ritual, but I won't give it away to those who haven't read the book. The point of mentioning this strange book and its evocation of a baby-less world is that it makes us aware of how much we need babies. And in the real world there is enough evidence of infertility in fish and many animals, and also in humans, caused by certain pollutants, to suggest that this fictional scenario is not altogether fantasy. We worry more about over-population, and that is a legitimate and serious concern. It is, however, a concern often used to enhance the image of global agribusiness corporations that offer to feed the world in return for controlling and manipulating the world food supply, or to justify bullying poorer nations—and of course mostly the poorest within them—into measures of population control they have not chosen. Human fertility has also, in many times and places, been twisted by demands for male babies to carry on a dynasty or just to prove you can father sons. Baby girls in many cultures used to be exposed to die and now may be aborted. Women have had to prove their right to exist by bearing many children. But even when children are treated as prizes, or possessions, or burdens, the birth of a baby is an event of amazement. Even after a difficult labor a woman can laugh as the child slithers into the waiting hands—it is a moment of sheer joy. And many a man who thought he didn't care much for children finds his mind and heart gripped by strange new feelings of awe, humility, and even fear, for the new creature is so small, so easy to hurt, yet so packed with life. This strange little being can focus a power of protectiveness, an energy to save and nurture, that extends far beyond the parents. A society like ours that easily closes its mind to the statistics of poverty can be shaken—for a while at least—to realize what that means in terms of children hungry and homeless. Harm done to children moves us to rage far greater than harm done to grown people, and photographs of weeping refugee children or infants dying for lack of food bring a response that general statistics of need and death cannot stir.

People may have babies for many kinds of either adequate or selfish reasons, but we need them anyway. A baby is a kind of resurrection, a new life that seems to say, "the failures, the hatreds, the deathly things, can be overcome. There is a future." Of such is the kingdom of heaven, and an incentive to try yet again to clean up some of the messy kingdoms of earth so they may become at least a little bit heavenly. I definitely believe in babies, a gift to choose with joy.

Grandmother

I think that, logically, the chosen gift called "Families" ought to follow one on "Babies," but something else kept coming into my mind, obviously connected to babies, but in another way. I have a reproduction of a lovely icon. It is named, on the back, Theotokos of Korsun. It shows the Mother holding the serious, mature-looking Child on her arm, and he holds a small scroll in his hand, in such a way that it seems to be coming from her mouth. Living with this one, I know why icons are more than just holy pictures. It has an extraordinary power in its serenity and quiet.

To me, the woman in the icon is not so much "Mother" as "Grandmother." This has something to do with my relationship with my own mother and grandmother, but also with the sense that the grandmother is one step further away from the mere practicalities of motherhood. Grandmothers are supposed to be wise, with gathered experience. They are supposed to have time. In real life, of course, many are as overworked and distracted as their daughters and some are obliged to be mothers to their grandchildren, but I'm thinking of grandmothers in folktales and stories, and of the long ago respect for the old women or "crones" who, before most people could read and write, carried the traditions of their people because of their long memories, and could say, "this is how it was done," and "that is what we believe."

So when I light a candle in front of my icon I name her "Grandmother." But she is not just the Christian Theotokos, the God-bearer, she is the age-old sense of the Woman who brings the god, who is the place of the god and the one from whose mouth the young god draws wisdom. (The old litany calls her "ark of the covenant" and "seat of wisdom.") I don't think of her as a separate goddess, but as what people have tried to express through so many images of goddess.

She is, for the Christian, Mary, the woman from Nazareth; tough, fearless, dedicated, not necessarily easy to get on with. But somehow she breaks out of that image. She is also and at the same time the one enthroned in vast mosaics in the domes of basilicas, or richly robed above the candles on altars, or carried in procession or standing in wayside shrines, a bunch of flowers laid at her feet. Pilgrims flock to her but she favors the poor and the unimportant. Grandmother, Great Mother, Virgin Athene, Mother Demeter, mourning Isis, Mystical Rose, Morning Star, Gate of Heaven. In all of this she is the one from whom life comes and to whom it returns, the Compassionate, the Comforter. Her eyes judge, and by her very being she refuses refuge to what is evil, yet she is Grandmother: available, immediate, the one who is always there, "refuge of sinners" (small ones and great ones are all safe with her if they repent), and "comforter of the afflicted" (whether a cut knee or great grief).

(At present, I haven't picked a "Grandfather" gift, not because I reject that idea but because I can't yet see it clearly, I'm still busy learning the Grandmother.)

There is more to Grandmother than herself, however great or humble, exalted or lowly. Behind and around her is someone else—not exactly greater but encompassing. She is Great-Grandmother. It is from her that the power and wisdom of Grandmother comes. She is like a vast atmosphere breathed out by the lives of countless people, women and men, whose lives have given life so that in the web of interdependence we catch, fleetingly, in images, notes of music, prayers, their exchanges of life. They are the great ones who sought and taught divine wisdom, who saw visions and dreamed dreams and often died for them, who lived life in God (or Goddess, it doesn't really matter) and not only with humans but with all that lives. This seems to me like a kind of life-giving mist, rising from creation, an atmosphere that all these beings breathe together. They "conspire" to wrap everything in power and hope. Through the mist we can discern the faces of some who are remembered—the Buddha, Miriam, Moses, Isaiah, Jesus, Mary, Muhammad, Benedict, Rumi, Hildegarde, Julian, Dorothy Day, Abbé Pierre and so many others past and also present. But also there are the millions whom few remember, but all of whom breathed together this atmosphere compounded of wisdom and compassion, which we must breathe or die. This, though so feebly describable, is for me "Great-Grandmother." From her the Grandmother emerges and steps toward us, touching and caring and guiding, telling stories, weaving, singing, reminding, warning, assuring, comforting.

Yet that isn't all. The more I meditated about this, the more clearly I saw that there is the Great-Great-Grandmother. Beyond the wisdom and fearsome beauty of humanity and of earthly living things there is the cosmos, and yet the cosmos is not only beyond, it is also within. The exchanges of being are in the molecules of our bodies and in the stellar dust clouds of utmost space. So the vast, unimaginably frigid distances where nebulae burst into life and die, and black holes contradict all the laws by which our imaginations have learned—these, too, are enfolded in the reality of our interdependent cosmos: Great-Great-Grandmother, ancient, boundless, encompassing, whose nature is compassion because that is what reality is, beyond imagination but as real as the taste of good food or the touch of kindness.

Grandmother, Great-Grandmother, Great-Great-Grandmother—they are also, of course, myself. How else could I exist?

One other thought lingers: perhaps space-time is curved because it is embraced.

Families and Friends

*A*ny kind of grandmother—even the cosmic kind—implies a family. It is awareness of the generations of families from a past lost in legends before writing, before genealogies, and reaching out to a future we cannot imagine but for which we have responsibility in our choices now, that gives the image of the Grandmother such power. This choice of gift therefore is possibly the most immediate, the most precious and also the most difficult of all.

My own family is at the heart of my life, of myself. Memories are of the two generations before me (and records going back many more generations) and of three generations coming along after me.

Families also are how the human family knows itself most profoundly in universal symbols. They have immense power because we resonate to them in the deepest of our family-linked selves.

So many of the strongest and most piercing images of faith—any faith—come from the experience of family. Symbols of Father, Mother, Virgin and Child, symbols of sexual love, of the Bride and the Lover, symbols of patriarchal dominance and biblical obedience—all these are the stuff by which religious devotion and religious structure are expressed. The emotional charge of these symbols, springing from such familiar and basic human experiences, provides much of the power of religious faith, for good, truly, but also sometimes for ill, because they can be used to manipulate as well as to comfort and encourage and heal.

This is partly why I have chosen as the first word of the title of this chosen gift "families," not "family." For us in the West, the word "family" is politicized, a word used by both churches and governments to persuade people to believe that the particular pattern of family life that has emerged in the West in the last few hundred years is not only the "normal" one, but the only right and "natural" one. The word "family" has been used to make women feel guilty and men feel inadequate if they don't conform to its stereotypes. It has been used to exclude men who love men and women who love women. It has relied on a carefully

edited version of history to uphold it—including the near-total ignorance of Christians of the fact that for centuries (up to about the twelfth
century) in Eastern Europe Christians accepted and blessed same-sex
unions with special liturgy. There have always been many kinds of families. Our familiar "model" can be wonderful but it is not the only one;
there are two-parent families but also one-parent families and "complex"
families of children from partners' former relationships. There are wonderful foster families! Family is a fluid concept and experience. It can
develop and change and is doing so in big and little ways.

Families are wonderful and terrifying, the best and sometimes
the worst human experience.

Having said all this, I want simply to celebrate families, including my own. Mine is a large one, not "typical," if there is such a thing.
We have twelve children—ten birth children and two foster children.
Bringing them up was an adventure. We made all kinds of mistakes but
somehow, through all the pain and struggle, they grew up into human
beings who are variously talented, loving, often tempestuous and always
caring. Our two foster children came to us from experiences they found
hard to speak about. All of us went through many moves from one home
to another, through poverty and through illness. Yet there was happiness
and celebration and learning—learning to make things and grow things,

to cook, to endure, to love and be loved, to care for each other and for others, not to be afraid to experiment, not to care too much about money (maybe not enough?).

Now, I am a grandmother and great-grandmother, as these men and women in their turn make families and go through the turmoil and fun and devotion and passion, and make the mistakes and some relationships fall apart and others grow strong as trees and there are new loves, and there is death and grief and children of their own, even grandchildren.

There were times, in those years when the children were small, when exhaustion seemed the only reality, and yet it was always possible to go on, and the children were delight and hope and fear all together. The morning face of a toddler is like the sun coming out, the busy "helping" of a small child is so beautiful it hurts. One of the most wonderful things in families is the recognition that, as the teen years come, one is meeting not a child but an adult, an equal: still a child in so many ways, and yet someone with whom one can, suddenly, share ideas, enthusiasms, dreams.

At this time in my life my "children" are companions, friends, people with whom I can share, people I can consult, whom I can admire and for whom I am grateful with a kind of amazement that these wonderful people began within me, or came into our life, and survived our failures and perceived our love through it all. Yes, I perceive and grieve over their failures and salute their courage in working to overcome them. We don't always agree, and I doubt if we would want to share a home. But—it all matters, it is all a source of hope and joy.

Out of this one experience of a family I want to salute all families that love and struggle and cry and laugh and learn. Out of this experience I grieve for the countless families so damaged by poverty, by abuse, by alcohol and drugs, by recognized or unrecognized mental illness, by the distortions of false morality or ambition or greed, and so many more evils—that the joy is wiped out, for children raised in fear or taught to hate. I celebrate those who, against what seems impossible odds, emerge as hopeful and loving human beings and try, with God knows what struggles, to create a better family in their generation.

Out of this experience I celebrate those who came before me, the stories I heard and the stories I shall never know, stories of adventure, of making money and losing it, of marriages and divorces, stories of lives so different from and so like my own, part of history and part of me.

Through those families who came before I am connected, back through the centuries, to the countless other families, of other cultures and other races, in the time when humanity was young. No wonder family history fascinates people, it is about the millions who lived and died and are forgotten but who through the millennia shaped the places, the customs, the possibilities, of particular families now. Photograph albums, inscriptions on gravestones, old letters, family legends: these things are so moving because they remind us who we are, in the unfolding of life, which happens because of families.

There is something else, linked to families yet, perhaps, ultimately more important: friendship. I put it here with families rather than as a separate gift, because one important thing about friendship is that it makes good families. What makes families good is not the blood relationship but the friendship that develops—the shared memories, griefs and jokes, the common experiences and values. Friendship is what makes a marriage or a partnership last, and it can outlast divorce. Friendship binds siblings together, and lack of it separates them. Friendship integrates new members—foster children, and the partners and spouses of the next generation—into the family. Without friendship a family drifts apart and lives with alienation, even hostility. Friendships, also, can help heal the wounds of family divisions and disputes.

But friendship goes beyond family, in the narrow sense. For many, for whom family relationships have been anything from difficult to horrific, the discovery of friendship can be the discovery of life. Friendships can be family, beyond blood ties. For survivors of painful family situations friendship can be difficult—it is hard to trust again when trust has been betrayed by those to whom it was given—but when, gradually, friendship can form it transforms. It opens up the possibilities of love and hope. It cannot undo terrible memories but can make it possible to live with them and live with joy.

Families are what you come from, for good or ill, but friendship is what you choose, when you are fortunate enough to find it. Friendship has the same challenges and pains as family. It has to be worked at, and chosen again and again. Some friendships belong to a certain time of life and are outgrown; friendships can be destroyed, too. But real friendship is, of all relationships, perhaps the most divine because it's a pure gift.

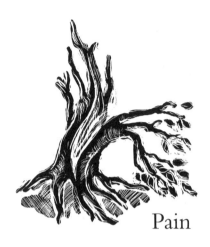

Pain

*T*he name of this gift to be chosen could belong with almost anything I've written about, because pain is part of life, including, inescapably, family life or friendship. It just seems important, now, to reflect on this reality which we must, since we cannot avoid it, embrace.

Nobody desires pain—to choose pain must, at first sight, seem perverse, even masochistic. But pain happens, it is unavoidable, and not only is it unavoidable, it is essential. Without pain nothing changes or grows. The pain of hunger leads to efforts to satisfy it, the pain of disease impels the work of healing, all art emerges from the pain of unsatisfied vision, craving expression. The pain of love is the subject of more poetry, novels, drama, than any other subject, and the pain of the oppressed drives the painful struggle towards freedom.

Pain and suffering are not necessarily the same thing though we often use the words interchangeably and indeed that is unavoidable. It is a complex distinction because they naturally overlap a lot, but for my purpose here I want to use them in distinction. Essentially suffering, in some sense, is what happens when we won't accept the pain as part of change and exchange that can lead to growth, a "birthing" experience. If we not only feel pain but are afraid and angry and resentful because we feel it, then we suffer, and the pain is worse. I explored this also in the part about sin, but here I want to express it another way.

Fear makes pain into suffering. Once, in the hospital myself in early stages of labor, I was in a room with a young woman who was in labor with her first child and in a lot of pain. She cried and screamed for help, and busy nurses could only tell her everything was "fine." She didn't feel fine, she felt trapped, and terrified at being seized by these monstrous surges of pain that she could not understand or escape or control. I, who had been there before, was able to sit beside her and hold her hand and gradually help her to relax, to breathe. As the contractions came I helped her to imagine (as I had once been helped to do) what the muscles were doing, slowing pushing her baby towards birth. With understanding, some of the terror let go; what was happening was no longer an attack, but the action of her own body, and she could go with it. The pain was real but no longer an enemy. She went to the delivery room soon after and I didn't see her again because I was sent home to wait!

The difference isn't that acceptance of pain takes the pain away, it is that we no longer suffer the extra pain of trying, uselessly, to fight it. One way of fighting it is by blame—it is someone's fault; I would feel better if the someone could be punished. (One reason for the popularity of the death sentence is that people think they will feel better if someone who has caused such pain is made to feel it. Actually, it doesn't work.) Another way is to feel guilty, "It's my own fault—what did I do wrong?" (There are always some to tell the lung-cancer sufferer that he or she should have stopped smoking.) If I made bad choices in the past, that affect myself or people I love, the inevitable results, the pain, are now. I can't change the past, I—and they—can only deal with the pain now. Rage and blame won't help but understanding and acceptance do. The pain doesn't go away, I have to live with it, but the "I" and "they" can become "we" and accepted pain can lead to growth and even to joy.

The pains of illness, of age, come to everyone. There is much we can do to find healing, to extend life, but the refusal to accept that pain will come, that an end will come, can cause far more suffering. People are sometimes persuaded into more and more desperate "treatments" because families—and doctors—are too afraid of their own mortality to accept the reality of disease, or simply of old age. The pain, for them, is not relieved, but made worse. The marvelous thing about the hospice movement is that it has helped both the dying and those who love them to accept what is happening. Keeping physical pain to a minimum allows the pain of separation to be accepted, not resisted, and there is peace and reconciliation and hope.

There are some pains we don't want to lose. There are little ones that are precious. I have a memory of an old house that my family once briefly owned. The house and the garden were not large but rambling and comfortable, with odd corners such as children love. It was sold long ago, for in 1940, being near the south coast of England, it was commandeered by the army. When, four years later, they left, our lives had moved on. For years I cherished dreams of some day, miraculously, being able to buy back that house. It is the kind of place in which good food should be cooked, children grow up, lots of visitors welcomed. I know I will never regain it, but I wouldn't want to be without that little pain of nostalgia because it becomes a kind of prayer that somehow there will be more places that are hospitable to children, and good real food, and friendships.

That is tiny. The pain of losing someone you love is incomparably greater, but precious. The memories hurt, evoking moments of shared joy, work, laughter, sadness. The memories hurt—but to lose the hurt would be to lose the joy, too. With time the pain gets less but joy and pain are inseparable.

To accept one's own pain is one thing, to accept the pain of others is something else. In a world wracked by horrible tragedy, how can we accept the pain of tortured children, people dying of AIDS, victims of famine and of deliberate terror? Surely to "accept" such things is wrong, evil, an abdication of our humanity? It is, if by "accept" we mean that we put it aside, shrug it off as nothing to do with us. On the contrary, the natural, right reaction surely is rage! That's right. That kind of rage at injustice is what drives movement for change. But not if it keeps on being rage, because then the drive becomes not one for justice but for revenge. The sustained, thoughtful, powerful action that brings about change may need rage to get it going, but then there has to be another kind of acceptance, when the pain becomes, in a sense, internalized, redirected, and the energy of it can work in whatever way we can towards change. Which may involve quite drastic life-style changes for ourselves.

I have only recently discovered some of these things about pain. There is so much to discover, and no lack of opportunity, because pain is a daunting reality. To be able to choose pain, to accept and grow, is a lifetime's work and perhaps only a few people learn to do it fully. Yet learning even a little makes a big difference.

Place

I think about, I choose, this gift called "place" not because it follows from thinking about the one just before it but because it is underneath—it "grounds" all our choices, our exchanges, our compassion. "Place" is our home, where it all happens. Places are holy ground—and I nearly wrote "holy places," but that separates some places from the others. I believe that place is holy, but that we need to recognize certain holy places—chosen or discovered—to make us aware of that holiness. So what is a holy place? How did it become holy? Often the holiness comes out of the mist of legend, told in the stories of people who knew about the holiness long before history, before dates and the writings of people who regard bits of land as possessions, to be bought, sold, and killed for.

Ancient peoples in many places tell the stories of the ancestors, the gods, who formed the cosmos. For Australian Aboriginal people there was the "dream time," when the land was shaped. To them, all the land is holy, but certain places are the focus of holiness, special places to experience oneness with earth and spirit, to seek wisdom and vision.

"Place" is both simple and very complex. When people have lived in a place for many centuries it absorbs the history of those years. But why did people choose to come there, build there and worship there? Did they choose it for practical reasons—the presence of good water, good building materials (wood, stone, clay for bricks) or because they felt some power was there of old gods and spirits? Or both. At one point on Hadrian's Wall that the Romans built right across the north of England to keep out the wild Picts, there is one large fort built slightly off the main line of the wall. It was just right for their purposes, a good place to build, with all the resources they needed. But the Romans called the place by the name of a local British god, whom they had adopted, as they often did. So was he there already? Was this a holy place? So was there not only practical sense but spiritual power in the choice of place? Do human beings choose places, or recognize them?

In the Andean mountains, peasant people still recognize holiness in every field, each is spirit-protected and made fertile, and the crops grow from that holiness and the wise people are attentive to the signs that guide the sowing and harvesting, and give thanks to the holy ones from whom comes fertility of human and beast and field. Did the people bring the holiness or find it? And so what is holiness in a place? Surely it isn't something separate from the practically useful qualities of the places where humans choose to live. Because, at least until recently, the place where people lived was also the place where they worshipped and they chose to live there because it was worship-ful, they recognized a blessing in it, that would protect and feed them.

The English settlers in New England felt God had given them the land they occupied, much as the ancient Hebrews did. (And both were ruthless about getting rid of competition for its use.) Long before that, the old Celtic peoples knew the divinities of mountain and stream and field, and their names later became attached to Christian holy men and women, from whom, as from the old ones, came blessings for hearth and byre and boat and field. Prayers for milking, for butter-making, for the traveler and the homecoming, for the kindling of the fire and its covering with ash for the night—all these were being used only a few generations ago, as Mary and Bridget and shining Michael and the kingly Christ were called to serve and protect the household.

People still go on pilgrimage to holy places, places where gods or saints have lived or taught or are buried. Pilgrims go seeking the power of healing in the place, or just to experience the awe of divine presence. Some of that presence will remain with the pilgrim, and be carried home with the memories and the souvenirs: water from Lourdes or the Ganges or the Jordan, a chip of stone from Jerusalem, a cockleshell from Compostela, holy bits and pieces, including plastic ones. And even the ways to such places, and home from them, are made holy by all the feet that trod in faith and fatigue. (Perhaps buses and planes can get impregnated with some of the holiness, too?) Shrines and temples are built, unknowing, on the sites of more ancient holiness, and the sounds and smells and sights of worship, as well as the carving and color and spaces, celebrate hidden and ancient and buried divinities as well as the newer ones.

But the holy places should help us to know and celebrate more intensely the holiness of all places. They are not exceptions, but reminders that the power we invoke in the sanctuaries is the power that binds us in eternal exchange of being with all that is. The blasphemy that turns the land into "property," valued only as a "resource" to be "developed," has for centuries and is still very literally killing men and women all over the world, as they are turned off the land they nurtured and that nurtured them, and driven into factories, or to work on factory farms that pollute and poison. The blasphemy is also killing the spirit ever more widely, as people are isolated in cities built for profit not culture, without common spaces, or are driven across the globe by greed or by sheer necessity of survival, cut off from genuine neighborhood and encouraged to dull the pain with more and more consumption.

In some places, tragically, the killing is more direct, when people who passionately love their place cannot live in peace with others who also have roots there. The place of the ancestors, the tradition, the whole way of life, become reasons to kill and torture and drive out those who share roots in the place. It has happened through centuries—the Bible is full of it—and it is happening now as horribly as ever. This long history is proof of how much "place" matters but also of how the idea of place can be perverted. Can people find a way to keep the passion for place and yet share it? Is the dulling of spirit that no longer recognizes the meaning of place the only way to stop the lethal possessiveness? It seems there are two enemies of holiness of place—hatred and suffocation.

Some people are beginning to recognize the suffocation and work to lift the stifling fog of consumer cultures. They want friends and neighbors, not shopping malls; they want—and begin to demand—neighborhoods where people can walk or bike to school, work, stores; they want green spaces. They plant gardens in cities on empty lots. They demand healthy food in such numbers that astonished governments and corporations reluctantly bury a few of their lies and begin to supply it.

But also in the places of hatred there are more and more who know you can't keep places holy by killing. They come together across divisions to share a vision of a place in which separate traditions can find a way to cherish the same land. They have a long struggle ahead but they experience already the vision they work for. So people demand places to be together, to bring up children together, to grow food—if not together then in ways and places they know as good. They want to learn their differences and celebrate them. When the places of human living are desecrated by hatred or by suffocation, the people die. We want our place, we want the right and power to make our place, our many, particular, different, varied places that are yet all one holy place.

Earth

The ultimate "place" for humans is the holy earth, but earth is more than a place. "Earth" can mean the planet, or the stuff you plant seeds in. Earth is one of the three essentials for life, the others being air and water, but we are curiously ambivalent about "earth." Other names for it are "soil" and (in the U.S.A.) "dirt," and we can talk about "good soil" or "good dirt" but also about "dirty" behavior or about "soiling" a reputation. Are we, at some level, afraid of the earth from which we come and to which we will return, afraid that our inescapable "earthiness" will break through the patterns of good behavior humans have devised to protect themselves?

This may be less superstitious than it seems. "Earth" *is* danger-ous. If we mistreat the planet it takes revenge on us, as we are discover-ing more dearly every year. And earth—the dirt, the soil—is wild and capricious; gardeners and farmers spend their lives either coaxing it, lis-tening to it, feeding it, anxiously waiting to see what it will do—or bul-lying it, forcing it, exploiting it.

In that wonderful children's book *The Secret Garden,* the orphaned, alienated, lonely child Mary asks her uncle, "Can I have a bit of earth?" She doesn't want the huge, planned gardens of his estate to wander in but the little, secret bit she has discovered, a place where she can dig and plant and uncover and watch things grow, and grow herself. The whole story is about the unfolding of the lives of two children, Mary and her invalid cousin, as the buds unfold. They learn to get their hands dirty—soiled—and to laugh and to trust. Their little world is our little world, and we need, like them, to learn the earth, both the planet and the stuff on the farm, in the garden or the window box, and under the forests and the wild places.

I believe we need to feel passionately about the earth, in both senses. We are made of it, it is our past and our present and our future and it is amazing stuff. Humans can—and do—render the earth barren, or treat it as the Nazis treated women from whom they wanted to breed the perfect race. All of this is going on, and it is all quite "scientific," but we have too long and too easily accepted that "scientific" means "detached and objective," nothing to do with feelings. Now, many scientists themselves know this is not true science—dishonest, because research can be motivated and therefore skewed by ambition, or arrogance, or the demands of profit, rather than the desire for truth. (After all, research is about finding the answers to questions, so it depends on which questions are allowed to be asked, and for whose profit the answers are intended.) We do indeed need to be *truly* scientific in our attitudes to the earth—the planet and the soil—and that, we now know, means being sensitive to it, studying it with radical honesty that is open to discoveries that may not be what we want to hear. The real scientists—and there are many—stand in awe before the realities of earth. The vision that comes from awe, love, care is a clear vision that sees what is there, not only what is quickly exploitable.

Our ancestors who worshipped the earth understood it better than we do. The vast and intricate complexity of earth, from its outer atmosphere to the last molecule of soil, is indeed full of divinity. But even if we live in cities—perhaps even more if we live in cities—we need to have earth and grow things in it and have green spaces and cherish them. We need to do this not just to have flowers and lettuces but for our salvation, for our spiritual survival. The "Gaia hypothesis" proposed that the whole earth is an intricate network of interdependent living systems, a whole and live organism. The truth of this becomes more and more evident—and the truth is scientific, and it is awesome and terrifying and wonderful. It could be the death of us, it can be the life of us, if we choose to believe in Gaia and give her the reverence and—yes—adoration that is due to the source of our life. When we touch earth we touch life, history, possibility. To touch earth should be an act of worship.

Gardens

his book uses the image of choosing flowers, which are themselves gifts of great price. Flowers live in wild places, but humans
have taught them to grow in gardens, too. So this is about gardens.

Earth is awesome, vast, worshipful, but through the ages people
have related most closely with the earth through the little bits of it they
know directly and personally. As hunter-gatherers we knew it intimately
as the source of food, for spirit as well as for bodily survival. As cultivators
we have worshipped, tended, grumbled at and celebrated the little fields
and orchards from which food came and in time, as cultivators, we were
tempted to think we could control the earth and subject her to our own
purposes. Gardeners, however, don't do this. "In the beginning," so the
story is told, God planted a garden as the appropriate place for humans to
dwell, and a garden is more than just any cultivated area. A garden is a

"paradise," which originally meant a royal park, tended not just for food but for beauty and enjoyment. The great seventeenth-century gardener John Parkinson made a Latin pun with his name, calling his book *Paradisi in Sole, Paradisus Terrestris* (Park-in-Sun's Earthly Paradise). He felt, with countless other gardeners, that the little patch they cultivate becomes a meeting place of heaven and earth in which, indeed, God might be found walking in the cool of the day. Whether it is a container garden on a balcony or a cottage garden or the elegant design of lawns, yew hedges, resplendent borders of some famous house, a garden is a place where human beings do a kind of dance with nature, not letting nature go as wild as the whim takes her but drawing her into patterns and unexpected encounters, yet never suppressing or coercing her. It's true some public gardens come near to coercion, with rigid patterns of regimented color, but even these can only make their flashy effects if the plants are well tended, and they do have a certain swaggering splendor.

Gardening is hard work and it is an art-form—one of the most difficult because the medium is so unpredictable. What musician has to worry about the weather, or what painter—unless of course it rains on his water color? As a gift to choose, gardening is whimsical, both a delight and a burden. Gardeners aim at the impossible perfection, always aware of what hasn't been achieved. They are addicts, evoking hallucinatory visions from seed catalogues and unable to pass a plant nursery without "just having a look." But gardening is also a spiritual discipline. It requires enormous patience and a willingness to accept failure and then to try again; it has a vision of the future, not just of next year but even of future generations; gardeners plant orchards and avenues and hedges, plantings that won't mature until long after the planter is dead. Gardening can be a consuming personal passion, an act of selfless love, a ritual of worship and praise.

At this time, when so many wild places are being destroyed, when everywhere threatened forests are disappearing, some gardeners are aware of a further dimension of gardening, and gardening magazines write about "wild gardens," about keeping part of even a small garden as a sanctuary of wildness. As butterflies and birds and small animals die for lack of the protection and food supplies of hedges and woods, gardeners try to create a miniature wilderness, or even a big one if they have space. They grow plants for bees and butterflies and dense bushes for tits and robins and field mice. They keep derelict sheds for owls and swallows.

When I think of this (and try to do it!) I remember that Tolkien wrote in *The Lord of the Rings* about those strangest of all the races of Middle Earth, the live tree people, the Ents. They tend and guard the forests, and are as slow growing and slow changing as the trees themselves. They are roused to rage—and action—by the wanton destruction of trees, and then they have power to smash human structures and return them to wasteland. (This, indeed, trees do, in the end.) But the tragedy of the Ents, so Treebeard the Ent tells his Hobbit guests, is that they have no one to come after them, because the Entwives have gone away and there are no Entings. For, long ago, the Entwives became less interested in "the great trees and wild woods and the shapes of the high hills." Instead, the Entwives "gave their minds to the lesser trees and to the meads in the sunshine beyond the feet of the forests. They saw the sloe in the thicket, and the wild apples and the cherry blossoming in the spring and the green herbs in the water lands in summer, and the seeding grasses in the autumn fields." But they did more than give their minds to these things, they began to "order" them. They became gardeners, making things grow "according to their wishes." When a time of "darkness" and war destroyed the gardens the Entwives moved further away and planted again "and the land of the Entwives blossomed richly . . . men learned the crafts of the Entwives and honored them greatly." But the Ents still wandered far off in the wild places and so, gradually, they lost the Entwives and could not find them in all their searches.

Indeed, for many centuries, people feared and even hated the wild places and when they made gardens they were enclosed, planned in geometric spaces, marking off the uncontrolled wilderness from the orderly richness of human cultivation. Yet when the industrial revolution began to give the sense that humans may control nature (and lay waste to a great deal of it) one reaction was the deliberate creation of "landscapes" instead of formal spaces, of "shrubberies" and the romantic cult of "cottage" gardens. So, now, as our culture poisons or cuts down more and more wilderness, perhaps the Entwives are beginning to regret their separation from their long ago wild lovers.

Perhaps the gardeners, making small wildernesses on the edges of their gardens, where they allow trees to grow, are creating small spaces for the reconciliation of the Ents and the Entwives.

These spaces are really neither wilderness nor garden, but both. Nurturing a reconciliation is a delicate business and will not happen on its own, so the little, new wild gardens and tiny woods need protecting from enemies, whether Orcs, rabbits or developers. Societies and organizations create larger wild gardens, which also need the care of gardeners who plant and protect. I wonder if, after all, in some distant future, Entings will be born who care for gardens and fields and forests alike.

Paradise is an elusive place, a part of earth and a state of mind, a divine-human collaboration. It is, as always, vulnerable to human stupidity. We have persuaded ourselves that it is impossible, a mirage. But that is because it requires the letting go of hatred and fear and greed and empty ambition and we are sure we can't do without those. But perhaps we could. . . .

Colors

$\mathcal{A}$ ll the colors of the rainbow can be found in a garden, but it was indoors with the door shut (he was a very private person) that in 1660 Isaac Newton used two prisms bought at a local fair to explore how all the colors of the rainbow are held within white light. He said there were seven colors, rather than the five which had been the usual count. But seven was an important number to Newton, who inherited a long tradition of perceiving number as itself sacred and mysteriously significant. Seven planets (though the telescope Newton improved would upset that number), seven days of the week, seven gifts of the spirit and seven deadly sins, seven notes in music (unless one were Arab or Indian), and there had been seven sacraments until the Reformation cut that down to two. (The sacraments had once been numbered seven for their sacred symbolism, even if it meant dividing baptism from confirmation from each other and clipping the status of marriage.) So, seven colors of the rainbow.

Yet, if you look at a rainbow there are many more than seven colors, as they shade into one another, and we search for names for all the subtle shifts. No wonder the rainbow was a divine sign. Even when we understand that white light is refracted into colors, the rainbow arc, brilliant against the still-stormy sky, can stir us to awe. It is a symbol of the unreachable, a bridge to nowhere or anywhere, yet a recurring assurance that there is peace beyond the storm.

Since Newton we have learned much more about why we see colors; even a child knows about the purple hidden in the yellow or the red in the green, and that a red light makes red disappear. It is almost frightening to realize that colors are, literally, an optical illusion; we see an object as colored according to the wave length it reflects because it absorbs all the other wave lengths. And not all creatures perceive the same range of colors that we do—they see what they need to see.

I suppose that for most purposes we could manage with a monochrome world. Black, white and some grays. From a very practical point of view it might seem that with that we could see everything we need to see. But it sounds, well, uninspiring. So I'm glad we have colors. They add daily delight, but much more than that. Even at a practical level colors have powerful effects on our minds—it seems we really do *need* to see colors. It has become commonplace that the colors people choose for their homes and their lives not only express their personalities but affect their moods. That's why choosing paint is difficult and can cause tensions and sometimes be a gesture of independence for a teenager!

Colors have stories, too. The "imperial purple" that at one time only Caesars could wear was made by crushing a mollusk called murex, and of course in the end everyone important wanted it and paid for it and fortunes were made, but its value also inspired the creation of a very few precious gospel books of vellum dyed purple and written in gold ink. Fortunes were made, later, from indigo, but the Indonesian tribal workers who stood in the vats, beating the indigo plants to release the color, did not make any fortunes at all. (The history of color is a history of beauty and invention but also of exploitation.) Cochineal beetles used for red dye will only feed on a particular kind of cactus. The orange varnish made in Cremona for Stradivari violins is supposed to enhance not just the tone of the wood but the sound the violins make. Precious lapis lazuli was dug out of remote mines by miners living in lonely celibate villages.

In this choice of gifts, of things that are sources of life and grace, I have included colors because, as I get older, the visible world around me seems more and more amazing and precious. The visible world also seems transparent to the spirit which is not separate from it but is its essence. Colors—the colors of flowers that inspired my image of the chosen wreath, the summer sky that draws one upward, the translucent green of young beech leaves, the velvet, purple darkness of night, the flush of a rose or a child's check—these endless varieties of color and tone are, in the end, the revelation of the light we can't see, the white light which the prism refracts: all things visible from the invisible, all from emptiness, everything from nothing.

Mystery

$\mathscr{T}$he mystery I am choosing here is not the unwinding of clues to a crime (much as I enjoy detective stories) or even the mystery, the strangeness, of so much of life and spirit, such as I've touched on in these reflections. The gift I choose here is different: the wonder of a craft or skill.

A "mystery" once meant a particular trade carefully taught and learned over years: "mystery, (archaic) a craft, or trade," the dictionary says. This "archaic" meaning once referred to the secrecy with which the trade guilds protected certain processes and ingredients of a trade from the non-initiated, and from inquisitive competitors. But those who learned the secrets, after long stages of practice, also had the sense of sharing a mystery in the other sense: there was a kind of awe at being part of a transformation, as one kind of being became something else—a tree became a chair; iron became a ploughshare; marks on a page became music; raw wool became a coat.

Learned skill does have this quality of mystery; the mixture of intellectual learning, practice and intuition that makes a good pianist or plumber or electrician or dentist or teacher or farmer or carpenter is extraordinary, awesome. Perhaps researchers into brain function can help us to wonder even more at it, for the experience of acquiring such skills, and even of seeing someone exercise them, is indeed a mystery.

Recognizing this quality of mystery in arts and trades makes it possible to recognize that all work that is good has—or should have—the same quality. Personally I dislike housework (with the possible exception of polishing good wood) but I dislike it a lot less if I can try to be aware of it as also a kind of transformation, a bringing of order out of chaos, a truly divine mystery if I could appreciate it! Doing household shopping also requires skill and practice, foresight and organization, if it is not to lead to a lot of waste and endless extra trips. To shop skillfully can save money, support farmers and manufacturers who care about the earth, ensure good meals and good health. Considered like that, it is a mystery to be learned and practiced with pride.

Dealing with money is certainly a mystery in a lot of senses. It is a necessary and wonderful service but even more open to abuse than most skills; as we know all too well and see daily in the news, necessary secrecy quickly becomes a way to defraud rather than defend. But to watch a skilled accountant at work is to witness a process of ordering and shaping and illuminating one of the essential elements of everyday reality.

Of all the daily mysteries, raising children is the most awesome. It is a skill learned and relearned; it is never done. With wisdom passed from generation to generation of parents and teachers, and in the passing corrected and adapted, it is the most essential human skill, the hardest to learn, the least rewarded. Women caring for children at home, and stay-at-home fathers too, are told (and themselves say) that in that time they don't "work"! In some places fathers as well as mothers are (often grudgingly) allowed to take time off from "work" when a new baby arrives, which is the least they need to begin to learn the mystery. And parents are blamed for not parenting right, when they have never been taught, or mostly taught wrong, the ancient and essential mystery of their craft. A newspaper article recently described one way of passing on the mystery of child-raising in Africa, in this case the mystery of the preparation of young girls for sex and marriage. In the tribal culture described, this used to be the special work of the aunt, the father's sister. As times changed and young people gained more education and social freedom the role of the aunt faded, but young women began to realize a lack, so one energetic aunt initiated a radio program and also gatherings in schools and homes, to offer advice in the old way. The mystery of raising a new generation can be carried on in new ways.

If we can believe deeply in the mystery of human skills that bring beauty and order and prosperity and a future, that will help to release the holiness in the things we do. It can give back the satisfaction and proper pride which is the right and due of every one who practices a mystery.

Ritual

I choose the gifts, like choosing flowers, and I weave them into a wreath, and discover how much they are truly a wreath; they complement one another. The connection is as lovely and complex as the flowers, such as earth, food, mystery, Christmas, and even grandmothers. Ritual is involved in all these wreaths.

Ritual is a series of actions, and often the words that go with them, which affirms the special importance of some human experience. Ritual is usually repeated, often or seldom, and although special one-time rituals are sometimes created, it is repetition that signals that what is ritualized matters as a continuous element in human life. Ritual is "religious," even when it is about very ordinary unreligious occasions, in the sense that it makes these occasions into times and places of significant human meeting and sharing, occasions which, when they are neg-lected, leave a sense of something important lost.

The setting of a table for a meal, and the cooking and serving and eating of a meal, are rituals that bind people together, symbolize the life this group of people shares as they share food. To refuse to eat with someone is to refuse to recognize a common humanity; to share food with a guest and then attack him was once considered the worst of crimes because it violates the meaning of shared food, which is shared life. Families whose members eat from the refrigerator and seldom sit down together very quickly loosen the bonds that make them a family; if a small child misbehaves and is removed from the table, that is a sign to him or her that behavior which disrupts this special ritual is not acceptable. To belong to this group of people means to share its rituals, and the belonging shreds if the rituals are neglected.

Families have their own special rituals, for birthdays or festivals of many kinds, which celebrate who they are. Repetition renews the sense of belonging, and when the next generation carries on the tradi-tion this continuity means a lot. The special recipe, the familiar song, sig-nal the delight of family oneness. People preserve national and ethnic traditions, like St. Lucy's crown of candles from Sweden or the soul-food of African Americans or Christmas pudding in flaming brandy from England or the Yule log or the Day of the Dead. It is all about continuity and the celebration of ties in the present and with the past.

Some rituals are more obviously religious, though still rooted in the daily life and family and community, and the Jewish tradition is, in the West at least, the tradition with the richest and most carefully preserved rituals, from the High Holidays to the weekly Sabbath observance with its special blessing and meal; in households that keep kosher the ritual governs everyday meals as well. In recent years many Jewish families who are not "observant" have rediscovered the power of observing the Sabbath, taking real time to rest, share food, enjoy each other. It is sacred time and ritual.

Most obviously there are the great public religious rituals of many faiths, the times when both belief and identity are celebrated and renewed. The sense that belief is about choosing, and choosing again, is at its clearest when we realize how these great symbolic rituals are orchestrated with music and color and movement in order to move each person taking part to rediscover a truth too deep and mysterious to be confined by a statement of belief: Easter, Ramadan, great saints' days in many countries, Rosh Hashanah, Passover, Diwali, Kwanza. And in many places rituals which once carried great spiritual power still survive as folk customs and still are able to evoke not only nostalgia and pleasure but a lingering awe at knowledge and even grief at meaning lost. (Morris dances and Mummers' plays are among these.) In many American cities now, around the winter solstice and in spring and summer, an organization called the Revels re-creates rituals of the season from many places, in song and dance and story and joke and symbol. For many people who attend year after year this is the truest experience of what seasonal ritual is about, it allows us to know how ritual remembers, renews, celebrates, grieves, encourages and (consciously or not) worships the compassion and joy that are at the heart of all life. The Revels often perform a very old ritual called the Abbots Bromley Horn Dance. The first time I saw it, I watched these strange shadowy figures with antlers on their heads moving in circles and patterns to an old, gentle, repetitive tune and I saw, thousands of years behind them, antlered heads casting shadows on cave walls, as people long ago celebrated their kinship with the creatures they hunted.

I believe in the power of ritual because ritual links past and present and future, generations, tribes and nations. And ritual may, perhaps, be among the most significant ways to heal old enmities. The Olympic ritual was intended to do this but nationalist competition has almost neutralized that statement of international solidarity. The healing rituals must come from the grassroots, from the people who have suffered and can forgive and move to a deeper affirmation, not of uniformity but of the beauty of diversity. Yet there are rituals of hate, and rituals of war that glorify violence; these, and sometimes even the rituals of patriotism, are more about excluding others than about loving our land. In the face of these we need to reclaim the power of ritual that heals and celebrates, at home, as communities, remembering the dead of all nations and tribes, affirming the possibility of peace. When the bomb craters and the ruins are still smoking, and the dead are barely buried, even then it is not too soon to come together and celebrate the rituals of grief, of hope.

Without ritual we are not fully human.

Folk Religion

*O*n the feast of St. Joseph families of Sicilian origin in the New England port of Gloucester gather to celebrate.

St. Joseph and quite a few other saints preside from a huge shrine of flowers and lights, and there is a lot of food—lavish seafood cooked the way mothers and grandmothers have prepared it for generations and wine to go with it. It is a cheerful ritual, mixing piety and good food in a way characteristic of the kind of religious celebrations worldwide that, without in any way rejecting official religious doctrine, spill over into homes and streets.

"Folk religion" is a tourist attraction in many parts of the world, because it is typically colorful, flamboyant and—to people accustomed to the more staid rituals of Western established religion—strange and even outlandish. But although it occurs in all kinds of religious contexts, it is only in Christianity—in practice almost always Catholic—that it is easily distinguished from the official rituals of the church. It may be countenanced—even blessed—by the clergy but it belongs essentially to ordinary people.

Such folk religion flourishes mostly among people with a strong sense of place—mountains or seacoast, desert or forest—whether they still live in their ancestral places or have carried the traditions of those places to far-off countries and urban spaces. It is, strictly speaking, "pagan," meaning the religion of country people once regarded as "pagan" (the "pagani," unsophisticated, primitive, uncouth) by sophisticated urban or landowning Romans.

After the Second Vatican Council of the Roman church there was a great zeal to clean up its act—at least its public act. A vernacular liturgy was to replace the obscurity of Latin; the priest was to face the people at Mass; everything was supposed to be clear and visible and open.

One thing that the enthusiasts for liturgical renewal were anxious to clear out, or at least up, were things called "devotions." These were rituals (popular, it was said, with old women) that distracted people from a proper appreciation of the beauty and clarity of the official liturgies: Novenas, "Benediction," May processions, prayers after Mass, rosaries-at-Mass, St. Philemona and other dubious saints.

In newly built churches there was lots of light and very few statues. There were no dim little corners with banks of candles, let alone statues that lit up when you put a coin in a slot! Of course these things survived in many places but they were regarded by the new liturgists as rather embarrassing survivals.

What has puzzled the liturgical enthusiasts is that the renewed liturgy has not, in practice, taken the place of the old devotions. The old women don't come to it any more than they did before, but neither do the young ones or the men. The huge gain of the recovered and renewed ritual is that the great, ancient symbols of fire and water, life and death, have been celebrated in many places with new beauty and care and deep love, symbols so old and new and so powerful they cannot fail to capture the heart. Yet when, as happened in Boston in 2003, the leaking seal in a double-glazed window in a hospital created an image that evoked a Madonna, hundreds crowded the parking lot to pray, week after week. Superstition? Ignorant credulity? Or the sudden eruption of a profoundly unsatisfied longing for the numinous?

This occurrence (and others like it, including claimed apparitions, weeping madonnas and more) is an expression of a sense that something—some holiness, some power—has broken through the surface of everyday life, and that power is loving, comforting, offering a sense of meaning, just as the processions and shrines do. Without in any way denying a God-centered faith, folk religion stirs the heart with experiences of divinity, mystery, holiness, through human beings who embody that mystery and make it, literally, visible.

As a young Catholic convert, studying art in 1947, in a Paris barely recovering from the years of German occupation, I was one among the huge crowd of students who went out from Paris to a vast suburban stadium to welcome Notre Dame the Boulogne, a beautiful modern statue of Mary standing in the bow of a boat as she was borne from city to city through war-scarred France. We sang "Chez nous soyez Reine" and knew her as comforter, sign of hope. We didn't analyze, we just knew we needed her.

It is true that the core of religious faith must be the commitment to justice which was proclaimed by the prophets of Israel and which is for Christians the irreducible heart of the gospel, but there is still the need, if we are to choose that commitment, to know a religion that deals with life at the level of myth, symbol, celebrations. We are "folk," and we lose a great deal if we become so solemn and pure that we are offended by the elemental, unrestrained, gaudy quality of "folk" religion. This doesn't mean that we can become uncritical, ready to swallow any tale of visions and admire local customs that may have become corrupted and manipulative. Folk religion can be oppressive too. We do need discrimination. But these rituals challenge our smug orthodoxies, religious or secular. They are crude, that means "raw," with the rawness of poverty and birth and death. The sad thing is that many of us—including myself—can only experience these rituals as strangers. We can learn that they matter, and admire them and yet not feel part of them at all. We have been away from home for too long; we can feel a deep nostalgia, even to tears, for a place we can't even remember.

Music

*T*he Shakers were extraordinary people. Their foundress was a blacksmith's wife, Ann Lee, who joined the sect of Shaking Quakers in late eighteenth-century England and inspired followers through her visions and preaching. She led them to New England, and these Shakers thought of her as Christ's second coming, in a movement that gave women full equality with men. In their heyday they attracted many converts and developed a unique lifestyle which left an inspiring legacy. Shaker men and women lived celibate lives in their elegant, austere and practical common homes; their furniture now fetches huge prices at auctions and is widely copied because of its pure and functional grace. But the Shakers made music as well as furniture and innovative buildings and machines. They made music for worship. They poured into their unaccompanied songs and their dances all the feeling and energy their disciplined lives kept strictly controlled. They called the songs "laboring," and the singing went on for hours and was indeed a labor of love. The music was their prayer. And they embodied music.

Music is at the heart of living in many ways and times and styles.

The cadences of Gregorian chant have, it is said, the power to lead the mind and heart towards contemplation and in every culture people have expressed in song, and in dances performed to the music of song, their deepest spiritual beliefs, hopes, and fears. In everyday life, through the centuries people have eased hard labor with work songs, as sea-chanties established the rhythm for raising the anchor or celebrated a hold full of fish. Music is part of all festivals in every culture and has enlivened repetitive jobs with songs we still treasure. People listen to music on the radio at work or in the street, to soothe or relieve boredom or escape unloved reality. More profoundly, whenever people are moved by a great common endeavor they have found words and music to express it and proclaim it. The mill-girls of Lawrence, Massachusetts, went on strike to the tune of "Bread and Roses." The unions sang, "Which side are you on?" The Marxists sang the "Internationale" and the Jacobins sang the "Marseillaise." The anti-apartheid movement was driven by song, and women's movements have their songs. The civil rights marchers sang, "We shall overcome," and they sang it, and a lot of other songs, on the way to prison and in prisons and it drove the guards wild, but it moved some of the guards, too. Music like this isn't just a proclamation to the world, though it is very effective; music draws people together in solidarity, and gives them hope and the strength to endure persecution, even death.

Singing together is one of the most joyful and satisfying things human beings can do, whether it is in a carefully rehearsed choir or a local chorus, or spontaneous singing at celebrations. In some places people still get together to sing for local festivals, like the May Day celebration at Padstow in Cornwall, and if that has become a tourist draw it is because the tourists find something there they don't find anywhere else. The Welsh sing at the drop of a hat or the raising of a beer mug. They sing in harmonies, in chapel, on strike, at football matches (it's amazing to hear a whole stadium break into harmonies) and in pubs. I wonder what it is that makes them do it but I wish the rest of the world would do it too.

At a time in my life when I had a lot of babies and therefore a lot of laundry (and the old kind of washing machine with no spinner) my small holiday at the end of a morning's work was to hang the laundry out on the line in the sun and wind. (Of course there were wet days, but that's another story.) And while I hung the sheets and shirts and small garments I sang. There was no one to hear, it was just a way to celebrate the day and work done and being alive. I sang folk songs and bits of opera and hymns, and if I couldn't remember the whole of a song it didn't matter.

There is something about music that is so fundamental to human beings that it can be dangerous. Hitler knew how to use music, and music can also reflect the deepest rages and hatreds, the passion for destruction, the longing for revenge for injustice. The darkness this music expresses exists. It is part of experience, it is a wail drifting through the streets of the cities, the sound of despair. Realizing how powerful the music bred by misery and hate can be makes us know how powerful all music is. It works at levels we don't recognize. Music can lower blood pressure and make cows give more milk. It can revive the spirit and allow us to let go of anxiety. It can bring hope and comfort.

Whether it is tapes in the office or humming as we clean or walk, or singing with children or in a choir, or playing instruments together or listening to them, music touches us. We need to believe in music and choose it with knowledge and love, choose it wisely because music can inspire and comfort and delight but it can also numb us with mindless syrup. Music can give courage but also encourage hate. Music can fill us with joy and enable us to grieve.

Recently an extraordinary performance of Verdi's *Requiem* was presented to commemorate the way that prisoners in a Nazi concentration camp had themselves organized a performance demanded by the guards as publicity to show how "humane" the camp was. In between sections of the broadcast performance two survivors of the camp told the story of how, inspired by their conductor, they found the will to rehearse and perform this dramatic liturgy of fear and grief, and through it to "sing what we could not say." Singing the doom-laden hymn of the "Dies Irae" they foretold the wrath of God to come, inexorably, on their persecutors. In the "Agnus Dei" they knew themselves as the lambs of God, innocents sacrificed by human evil. Heard in this way the meaning of this music erupted like a volcano of rage, pity, judgment and— somewhere beyond it—hope. Music can do this.

Long ago it was believed that the stars and planets were embedded in invisible transparent spheres that turned in majestic rhythm around the earth, and as they turned they made music which certain gifted people could hear. Somehow or other there must be music in the vastness of the heavens, as there is music in mountains, and in the seas where the whales sing, and who knows what other voices we are too limited to hear? There is music in the heart of us, and we need it and need to choose to liberate it.

Miracles

*I*t is not hard to believe in miracles. For one thing the word itself simply means "wonderful": a miracle is an event that makes people feel that the ground of reality is not as solid and predictable as we thought—it can break open and reveal unexpected joy. In this sense—and it is a very important sense—the first green shoots of bulbs pushing up through winter's earth have a character of miracle that is just as real though it happens every year. The cry of a newborn baby, the sight of a friend not seen for many years, the first sign of recovery from illness, all have this quality of miracle, they move us to wonder and joy and gratitude.

In another sense, though, miracles are events that can't be accounted for in any of the ways which we usually use to measure reality. A medical "miracle," for instance, is not just the discovery of an amazing new drug or treatment, "miraculous" as this may seem to people who unexpectedly recover health because of it. In the more startling usage, a miracle is the kind of healing that can't be explained by what we know of the processes of the human body. Virtually instantaneous healing of a cancer, or a withered limb that regains muscle use and function—such things are miracles in this powerful sense. They are so extraordinary that they cause people to rethink their notions of reality.

For some people the idea that events unexplainable by the usual disciplines can happen is too disturbing to be accepted because it upsets the sense that the world is safe because it is explainable. Indeed when a really extraordinary, apparently unexplainable thing happens, one way to deal with it is simply to say that we don't yet know enough to explain it, and given the extraordinary increases in scientific knowledge in the last century—still growing at a huge rate—this isn't unreasonable. The amount we *don't* know, for instance, about the human mind and its relation to the brain is colossal, and one day we may know a great deal more.

Personally, I am grateful for all kinds of miracles, and I don't mind if some of them prove more "explainable" than they seem at present. (A video of an ultrasound picture made in a Chinese hospital showed the disappearance within fifteen minutes of a large cancerous tumor in the kidney. The Chinese have their own explanation.) I think miracles of all kinds matter because they startle us into a radical experience of the beauty and complexity of life. They let us out of the cage of our preconceptions and fears and for a moment teach us a joyful humility about the nature of reality.

Some people have visions or have the gift of healing or "know" things most of us don't. Others don't have such gifts—or is it that we simply don't begin to grasp the potential of being human and that we feel safer without extraordinary gifts? Do some, by seeking or training or apparently simply by inheriting the capacity, transcend not so much "humanness" as the protective limitations that our humanity has developed through the ages in order to survive?

On the whole I'm content not to be one of those who transcend, but I am grateful for the miracles that show me how much more wonderful reality is than I can understand or experience. Of course I may know more when I'm dead.

In a sense, the purpose of this book is to nudge those who may read it into a greater willingness to perceive the miraculous, to be amazed, awed, even terrified, by a newly perceived reality in things we have taken for granted. Miracles of all kinds knock away some of our sense of being in control, they confront us with the limits of our understanding, an experience that can be disconcerting. But if we can accept the experience, it also extends our limits, reaching into areas where we aren't certain, aren't in control, yet enriched by a sense that we are also citizens of a wider realm that we share with many others. It is, we realize, actually our homeland.

Fairies

*I*n *Peter Pan,* when the fairy Tinker Bell is ill, and the children in the audience hold the power to prevent her dying, Peter asks them, "Do you believe in fairies?" and of course they all say "Yes" and she recovers. I'm not sure I believe in Tinker Bell, though as a child I helped resurrect her, but I think I believe in fairies. I don't mean the kind on Christmas trees or greeting cards, or even the charming fairies that each have their special flower in the children's books of Flower Fairies, which I still love.

To believe in fairies is somewhat connected to believing in miracles because it means believing in the possibility that we don't know all there is to know about this earth and its creatures, or about ourselves; it is to acknowledge that maybe there are powers and presences (or whatever one wants to call them) that might be glimpsed out of the corner of an eye, at least metaphorically, but when you turn there's nothing there. Some people are more aware of such things than others. I am not "fey," which is a Scots word for this kind of awareness of something-going-on-just-out-of sight. I can't see fairies, or "the little folk," or "the people of the hills," or similar beings called by any of the many names they have been given. I wish I could, and I am glad that some people can. Do the people who see fairies see the embodiment of old stories? Do their minds make pictures to give shape to a sense of something going on they can't define? Do fairies or other creatures put sixpence in the shoe of the kind-hearted? Do "they" remove warts or punish the malicious with bad luck or find lost children? Are "they" sometimes malicious if they are disbelieved in or driven out? Since they don't like cold iron, or unkindness or violence, we could do with more of them in some households.

Fairies are, however, more than those extra (to us) inhabitants of houses and fields. To me the importance of fairies is that they are fantasy. Fantasy is the creation of what has not been, what perhaps can never be, but which fulfills a deep need. Really good fantasy gives us entrance into a world that is richer and more exciting and often more dangerous than our usual one. It is an escape, for a while, from the limits we normally acknowledge but, as Tolkien told us, to escape need not mean a cowardly refusal to deal with reality. It is rather an escape from unjust imprisonment, allowing our imaginations to grow wings and fly away. With those wings we can also fly over lands that truly may come to be, for fantasy is also a tool to create symbols of a possible different future. Thus the real future can be enriched and even re-created by means of the power of those symbols.

In this way fantasy and reality have a symbiotic relationship: fantasy draws on reality to shape its symbols and the symbols (possessing a life of their own, yet one which we guide and nurture) have the power to shape reality if we so choose. But fantasy and reality are not the same thing, and to confuse them leads not to re-creation but to evasions of reality, or worse.

Fairies—or one of the many exotic beings of fantasy—are powerful in our own lives as individuals but also as societies. The wrong kind of fantasy with the wrong kind of beings in it can be horribly evil, as Nazism was, and all the sick little sects and cults that live their fantasies and are ruled by their evil fairies to the point where they can't tell the difference between fantasy and reality. But the fairies of right fantasy can have a power which becomes prophetic, and indeed the great prophets have always used fantasy to draw minds and hearts towards a different future.

So it seems there are, in practice, two kinds of fairies: the kind that are part of everyday life, if we let them and care to acknowledge them, and the kind that are "fantastic." In older or less "civilized" cultures (but that is a loaded word, and I put it in quotation marks to imply that "civilized" culture isn't necessarily superior) fantastic fairies and the kind that find your needle for you are sometimes the same, but mostly we don't have the imaginative insight to allow that possibility. Let us at least believe in the fantastic ones because they can offer us hope and energy to work for a different future. As for the others—if it is too much of a leap to *believe* in them, the idea of them can at least make us pause a little to acknowledge that there are many things we don't know about the world we live in.

Jesus

$\mathcal{I}$t is hard to write this bit. What does it, can it, mean to say, "I believe in Jesus"? The statement is at the heart of anything calling itself Christian, yet so much that is Christian seems to have little to do with Jesus. It is a statement that carries a heavy baggage of pietism and spiritual bullying and sentimentality. But there's no way to escape dealing with it.

I believe in, and choose, the gift of this amazing man who walked through cultural and religious walls as if they were cobwebs, and cried when his friend died and was depressed when other friends let him down, and really believed that he could get through to people and persuade them that they could live together in a society of hospitality and mutual support and justice. He could confront smug bureaucrats and be outstandingly rude to them on occasion. He liked all kinds of people, including a lot of women. He died because he was a menace to the stability of both the religious and the political systems, which as usual were not easily disentangled.

I believe in Yeshua who was a Jewish peasant and understood the relationship of the people to the land and was outraged at the way rich people took more and more land so that peasants who lost theirs could only survive precariously as hired hands. His teaching and his rage grew from the Hebrew prophetic tradition that condemned monopolies and huge wealth and saw true prosperity as the prosperity of land and people together, not the increased wealth of a few.

What else? Even to use the name "Jesus" stirs up vast clouds of old, old doctrine and devotion and battle—too often literal battle— between people who used the name in differing ways. Often all this seems to have nothing essential to do with the man from Nazareth. But it won't do just to say I believe in this amazing human being, because all the other stuff gets in between—and has to, because, without all that, who would remember an obscure victim of Roman tyranny?

There are the titles in the Christian scriptures—Son of God? Word of God? Savior? Redeemer? The images that have been used to express the extraordinary changes that this person brought about in the lives of millions are just that—images. They grew from the religious language of the times, and changed with the times. For many people the old images still work but for many they do not illuminate the reality, they bury it. What kind of extraordinary gift is this man? Can I choose that, and mean anything further than gratitude and love for the human being whose actions and words still bring hope, sanity and courage, inspire passion and offer vision?

I can make this choice because this very strange flower is indeed one in a wreath, and cannot be pulled out without damage to it and to the wreath. If I am able to choose such a gift, that is because there are other gifts behind and with it. There is the awareness that the universe is compassionate, and yet that in a world where there is so much weight of resistance to compassion it makes sense that the volcano of compassion has to break through the thick crust of selfishness, hatred and greed. Compassion must somehow be present where it has to be, among humans, who alone in all creation can choose to refuse and deny the reality of interdependence. What would one expect the forces of resistance to do in the face of such an outbreak of compassion as Jesus represents, raging and healing and changing people? They would do what they did, what they always do—try to crush it.

It seems it wasn't crushable. The thing that is claimed uniquely for Jesus is that he rose from the dead, and that is what has given momentum to all else that was claimed and taught and shared and preached and written about him since. At one time you either believed this or you weren't a Christian. Now, it is not uncommon to suggest ways to explain the faith that burst out among a small group of Jews as somehow separate from the stories of the appearances of the risen Christ, which are proposed to have been written later as ways to image such a transforming event in the lives of those who began it all. It is especially tempting to male scholars to do this because the earliest witnesses of resurrection, according to the gospel accounts, were women. Such a solution makes everything tidy and doesn't assault our scientific clichés or put us at odds with assumptions of modern Western culture.

I don't think we know enough about the nature of material reality to be so glib. That is, we don't know fully enough the implication of the scientific statement that matter and energy are interchangeable. There was certainly a lot of energy around Jesus, and the image I used of a kind of volcano of compassion breaking through and pouring into the world does at least suggest a very great energy. You can't put the lid back on that, and it suggests you might find it hard to keep the tomb closed.

Whatever images our time draws on to try to preach the mystery, we can never fully express it, anymore than the old ones did. And the old ones can sometimes be used, too, and make sense, if we let them *be* images and, as it were, go *through* them, sharing the search of our ancestors, clumsy yet amazed, knowing something that touched the deepest places.

I find it easier to use the old images—at least some of them and at least on ritual occasions—when I can trust the images that express for me something of this "Christ event," as the theologians call it. If compassion does break through the crust of apathy and greed and hatred, it must do so in ways that openly and explicitly contradict the values that make that crust so hard. It must raise up what has been brought low, and lay low what seems so high. It must call blessed the poor, the humble, the persecuted, because in such situations compassion has at least a chance. And, vice-versa, where you see this kind of thing happening—people healed and healing, forgiven and forgiving, fed and feeding, freed and freeing—then you may suspect that the compassion which is the nature of the universe is at work. Only something as strong as that could do it. If so, all kinds of strange things are likely to happen, even resurrection. And maybe women, who are generally less committed to the status quo since they don't do too well in it, are more likely to have a clue about what is happening.

To say, "I choose the gift of Jesus," doesn't mean to me that this event is the only time the volcano of compassion erupted. His eccentric follower, Paul of Tarsus, said he was "the first born of many siblings." At least for the Christian world he has been "first," but a person who described himself as a servant isn't likely to demand that kind of recognition. He was about smashing up the crust; it seems he maybe hoped there would no longer be any need for volcanoes because there would be no more resistance to the mutuality of compassion and joy which is the nature of the universe and which he tried so passionately to share. And as that hasn't happened yet, the passionate compassion in the universe takes every chance it can to break through. That began long before Jesus and is still going on, and will go on, which is about the only reason for hope, but a good one.

Atonement

*T*here is one word which has been used from the earliest days of Christianity to describe the difference Jesus, the Christ, made to humanity: atonement. Sinful, hating and hateful humanity was apparently trapped in an endless cycle of suffering—the fear of suffering and the infliction of suffering, of dominance and oppression and resistance and suppression—and yet a humanity in which the vision of compassion and justice and peace survived. Something, people always knew, had to break the cycle. God, it seemed, kept showing people what would make them happy and peaceful, yet they seemed unable to live by that vision except in brief bursts. The idea that something had to be done to put this right and that Jesus did this comes to us in the image of sacrifice—atonement. For me (and many others) this is an intensely difficult and ever repulsive idea, certainly not one I can easily respond to. Yet, it has been so central to Christianity I felt I could not leave it alone. In the end, something came to jerk me into a recognition of meaning in an unexpected way, and quite recently. But that is linked to the ancient beliefs and images of atonement, long before Christ.

The ancient, primeval notion was that the divine gifts that kept humans alive and prospering should be acknowledged as gifts, not possessions. The acknowledgment took the form of gifts in return—the "sacrifice" of some of the divine gifts to the divine power. For many ancient cultures, this was peaceful, a thanksgiving, a celebration.

There are records, only unearthed and interpreted in the last fifty years and still not easily acknowledged, of a culture of "old Europe," lasting several millennia until about 3,000 BC, which seems not to have known war, whose divinities—mainly female—were happy with offerings of food, including bread: the oven was itself a sacred thing. But this culture was buried by later ones whose divinities were mainly male and were warlike, and to be feared. To gain their blessing and avoid their punishments sacrifices were needed—not just food but animals and even humans. This idea is repugnant to us, we don't want to believe in a god who demands blood sacrifice. But (to simplify drastically) Christians, led by St. Paul, saw the terrible death of Jesus as a perfect sacrifice that ended the need for other sacrifices. It was a sacrifice out of love, and God was satisfied with it; His wrath was appeased—in this context the pronoun needs the capital letter.

For many—myself included—that image does not evoke awe, or gratitude, but repulsion. We can't live by a god who demands such atrocious suffering, one who is appeased by any human sacrifice. If God loves humankind, how is the destruction of one who is claimed to be God's beloved a fitting proof of that love? But if that imagery doesn't speak to us of salvation, but of ancient fears of a vengeful God, does that mean there is no sense, no meaning, in the images of sacrifice? For many, there is indeed no sense in it, it is alien and useless.

So, I found I had to see if I could discover something within this that warranted centuries of devotion—including the devotion of wonderfully loving and creative people whose lives were and are an inspiration, including many great mystics. If they found something divine and inspiring in this doctrine, then there must be something even for the unmystical dwellers in the twenty-first century, not adjusting easily to doctrine presented to us as a given. Eventually I began to feel my way into a kind of understanding, through reflection on a truly horrifying event that happened in England in 2001.

There was an outbreak of foot-and-mouth disease. Nobody knows for sure where it began, or even when, but it may have begun with pig swill made from restaurant food imported from a country where the disease was endemic. The pig farmer didn't observe hygiene regulations (too expensive) and shipped the pigs to market, where they infected other animals and were moved again to infect again. It spread rapidly, mostly because of the custom of transporting live animals over great distances and often through several markets. Stressed animals have less resistance anyway.

During 2001, altogether for at least twelve months of the epidemic, 4.02 million animals were slaughtered by government order: sheep, cattle, pigs. Less than 15 percent of them were in places where tests had been made that proved infection.

It matters to realize that foot-and-mouth is not usually a deadly disease and most animals, left alone, recover. They do not infect humans nor is the meat affected, but (like all sick creatures) the animals lose weight and condition, so they become less valuable and the loss in value is, in our world, what counts. (This has nothing to do with Mad Cow disease, which is always fatal and can be transmitted to humans.)

For months, the countryside was dotted with huge burning pits from which the reek of burned flesh drifted across farms and villages and into the towns. By day columns of smoke rose up into the sky and by night the fires of this holocaust could be seen for miles.

To what god were those innocents offered? The discussions and researches since then have made it clear that the rush to indiscriminate slaughter on such a scale was not proven necessary, nor did it really shorten the epidemic. What it did was to "satisfy" (yes, that old word for the reason for sacrifice) the gods of the export market and "appease" the investors. That was all it was about. Yet something quite different also happened.

As the news of the scale of slaughter spread, as people saw lush green fields empty of cattle, pastures with no grazing sheep, as the questions were raised and the motives exposed, there was a gathering anger, but also a heart-searching, a movement of sorrow and even guilt. Did we do this? people asked themselves. This was done in our name: Is this what we want—this vast destruction of the innocent?

For many, there was a change of heart, a new awareness of the values that control the way we get our food, a kind of repentance, and a decision to make different choices in the future. It wasn't enough, and it isn't even clear if, in case of another epidemic, things would be done differently by those who make the decisions. But, however you measure it, we can say that by this sacrifice some souls were "saved" or, to put it in the images of the prophet Ezekiel, some people's hearts of stone were changed to hearts of flesh.

The Lamb of God who takes away the sin of the world? Those who witness to that sacrifice have to recognize that the death of Jesus was the result of Roman (read, any controlling power) fear of loss of control, and there were not enough people who had the vision to recognize the roots of the decision for death, and the courage to stand up against it—understandably, given what the Romans did to those who opposed them. But those who understood, later, were changed. This death, as the story was told and the message spread, for the first time held up a victim of totalitarian oppression and political expediency as worthy not just of compassion but of overwhelming, awe-filled reverence. This victim was the one who had, after all, brought a vision of a transformed world. This death showed up the nature of the forces of evil at work, it demanded that people choose between good and evil, between death and life. Innocent death can do that. "The blood of martyrs is the seed of the church," it was said, and if the church itself has made plenty of martyrs, it is still true that the witness of those in any tradition who are willing to stand up against injustice and suffer for it, sometimes to death, can change hearts like nothing else.

For people of the West, however, there has to be the acknowledgement that its Christian-formed culture throughout its long history turned the cross, the hideous Roman punishment to which Jesus of Nazareth was condemned as a danger to Roman control, into a symbol of Jewish guilt for that death and so led inevitably to the Shoah, the holocaust in which six million of Jesus' kin died. It may seem shocking, even grossly distasteful, to speak of this vast genocide in the same breath as the slaughter of animals by panicky politicians, but the nearness, the almost "domestic" and "next door" character of the sacrifice of innocent creatures to false gods can allow us to recognize how, age after age, the innocent are sacrificed, their deaths are justified by lies and the idolatrous crime presented as necessity. And yet, somehow, truth gets through, it confronts and challenges and moves hearts and even changes history. We cannot say too loudly or often that nothing—no repentance or change of heart—can ever make good out of the huge evil of which the Nazi ideology and its servants were the ultimate agents. Such "sacrifice" to the gods of greed and domination can never be other than totally evil—and yet, when it happens, people may see, and hear, and change. It may take millennia to recognize the idolatry and stop denying and begin the hard process of repentance, and the Christian churches to this point have only hinted at real repentance, but it can and must happen.

There are also those other millions of innocents who died because of wars, or gunfire in the streets, or abuse at home, who never understand why they suffered, yet their deaths roused a public outcry of grief and repentance. These lambs of God are the victims of the sin of the world. May the changes that can follow take away just a little of the sin?

Martyrs who know why they suffer, slaughtered children, slaughtered animals—they are all victims of human sin. So can we make sense of this image of Jesus as Lamb of God? Perhaps we can let go of the image of the God who demands to be appeased by sacrifice and perceive, rather, the boundless compassion that, if it can drive a human being finally to accept the most horrible of deaths because the alternative is denial of the truth of love, is then also the very nature of divinity. There is, in such an experience of God, a deep and cosmic grieving that calls on humans to grieve too, to look at what we have done to make such things possible, and change, and choose another way. In the great mystery of interdependence, the pits full of burning carcasses, the slaughter of innocents in Nazi Germany and in Iraq and Afghanistan (and Colombia and Peru and Armenia and El Salvador and Vietnam and all the other places) can perhaps be recognized as one with the Lamb of God who stands, glorified, on altar frontals and banners, not because Jesus somehow supersedes or sums up those other innocent deaths but because this symbol is a perpetual reminder of the sin of idolatry and of the need for hearts to change.

Whether such sacrifice can take away the sin of the world is up to us. The terrible irony is that we have used that uniting symbol of love unto death as triumphant sign of exclusion.

Women

*F*or the past twenty years I have been part of an organization whose work, grounded in a mission of justice and hospitality, is very much concerned with helping very low-income (sometimes no-income) women find a way to a fuller life. Some are homeless with their children, but others—housed after a fashion—desperately need education to help them get a job that pays the rent. One education course they are offered is called "Foundations." It includes all the basic things the women missed out on—math, computers, writing and so on—but it also includes a weekly class in women's history. This is in some ways the most important of all, because they learn the how and why of their own situation. They learn that they aren't poor because they are bad or stupid, as they've been taught all their lives through subtle and not-so-subtle messages, but that the social system of the time and place has created the pattern of their lives. They learn about the struggles and triumphs of women who worked for suffrage, for so long that when the vote was won very few of the original suffragists were still alive to cast theirs. They learn about times when "wise" women were burned as witches for their knowledge of healing herbs, and married women could not keep the wages they earned and lost their children if they separated from an abusive husband. The women in the class learn about women who broke through, became doctors, architects, explorers, above all gained self-respect and hope.

The effect of this class is explosive. Women are amazed, excited, transformed! "If they could do it, so can I! I can study, get a job, even speak out in public about issues that affect us!" (And they do.)

Seeing this happen, and learning about the heroism of so many women who battle impossible odds for the sake of other women, their children, their country, I am awed and thankful, but also full of rage and sadness, because it is all too fitting that this choice, of the gift of women's lives, comes to me right after the choice of atonement as a flower—a dark rose, streaked as with the blood of the innocent.

The story of women is mostly untold and what is told (or discerned from what is told about men) is mostly horrible. True, there was that time, that I referred to earlier, those millennia ago, when the religion of the goddess gave women honor and leadership and there were no weapons of war and no big palaces or big temples but only small shrines and sacred places for childbirth—and those sacred ovens for the bread of life. It seems hard to believe, it was too vulnerable, it was wiped out by the people with warrior gods and lots of weapons.

In revenge or fear, the new gods made sure that the goddesses, and their peaceful offerings and their reverence for the earth and the body, and the women who symbolized all this, should be without power, and so it has been ever since, and even the emergence of women in the last 150 years has been partial and is still widely resented.

This gift that I am choosing now, then, is a perilous gift, and the women's story that is being partially uncovered is about the sacrifice demanded by gods with many names, it is about the sacrifice of women in wars, by rape and enslavement and slaughter. It is about the labor of women in mines and factories, dying young of disease and hunger. It is about the routine abuse of girls, along with their younger brothers, by fathers, guests, any powerful male, and later in life by husbands or even sons. It is about the lowest wages and dismissal from jobs for pregnancy, and so about prostitution and back-street abortion. It is about sweat-shops, and women preparing flowers for our markets who get sick from the chemicals used. It is about sex tourism and the trade in pornography, including the kind that requires killing, for the ultimate thrill.

Recently, a girl of sixteen was stabbed to death by her father because she secretly wore make-up and had begun to date a boy at school who was of a different religious background. The father was sent to prison for life, because this happened in England. In many places he would have been praised for thus avenging the family honor. It happens routinely. Women are still the sacrifices.

Whether the gods are called Honor or War or Trade or Religion or Family, they demand sacrifice and the sacrifice is most often (though God knows, not always!) female.

But, long ago, Isaiah the prophet wrote of a sacrificial victim whose guiltless suffering was not required by any god, but yet wrought a transformation. The words about the one who has come to be called the Suffering Servant are familiar to Jews, and perhaps they are about the fate and destiny of a whole people, but they have been applied by Christians to the sacrifice of Christ. There are other ways to read this great poem: some years ago, some friends and I, preparing a liturgy using this passage, chose to change the pronouns. This is part of what we read:

> "She grew up before the Lord like a young plant
> whose roots were in parched ground;
> She had no beauty, no majesty to draw our eyes,
> no grace to make us delight in her.
> Her form, disfigured—less than human.

She was despised, she shrank from the sight of men,
tormented and humbled by suffering;
We despised her, held her of no account . . .
Yet in herself she bore our sufferings,
endured our torments,
while we counted her as punished by God
struck down by disease and misery.
But she was pierced for our sins,
tortured because of our wickedness,
So the punishment she endured is for our health
and by her scourging we are healed . . .
. . . the Lord laid on her the guilt of us all,
she was afflicted, submitted to be struck down
and did not open her mouth
as she was led like a sheep to the slaughter . . .
Without protection, without justice, she was taken
away, . . .
. . . stricken to death for my people's sins . . .
though she had done no violence
and spoke no treacherous word."

That seems a fair enough summary of the history of women, but
the God who witnesses this horror does not welcome this sacrifice but,

grieving and outraged, reaches out to vindicate, to receive, to heal. This very different kind of God cared for the tortured victim and

> "... healed her who had made herself a sacrifice
>> for sin. . . .
>
> She shall see her children's children.
> . . . after all her pains she shall be bathed in light,
> After her disgrace she shall be fully vindicated,
> So shall she, my servant, vindicate many,
> Having borne the penalty of their guilt. . . ."

To read this passage through in such a way is a revelation, it rings with such a piercing note of truth. It isn't saying, I think, that the suffering of women is required by God because of human sin, any more than the horror of Jesus' crucifixion was desired by the Abba to whom he prayed. But it happened, and in both cases what matters is that those who witness it recognize it as evil, a blasphemy against all that is holy, just, right, human. When people can say, with conviction and deep horror, that it is obscenely wrong that a man be crucified for preaching justice and compassion, or that women (and all other innocent victims) be humiliated, despised, oppressed, exploited, and when enough people can then go on to do something to change the laws, the attitudes, the beliefs, that allow this kind of thing—only then will the horror become a sacrifice that can save, and the victims be "fully vindicated and bathed in light."

It is true, it happens. The amazing thing about getting to know the story of women and the stories of women is that in spite of all that the dominant cultures could do, through the centuries there have been women whose lives blaze with the light of vindication, who broke through the oppression and made peace and healing and justice and beauty. There are also the ones we can only guess at, whose names we will never know, who were the wise women and the teachers and the mothers and grandmothers who nurtured and cared and planted and grew and made homes, who made it possible for the men they cared for, too, to hope and to see a different world from that dominated by the gods of War and Profit.

The gift of women—of each woman—is a flower of unique strangeness and beauty, yet its power is that it shares beauty with all the other flowers and brings out the radiance of each.

Transformation

*L*ooking back through the titles of these chosen gifts, it becomes clear to me that many of them have one thing in common: They are about transformation. Compassion, prayer, mystery, miracles, resurrection, ritual, even food, earth—all these and more are about change that amounts to transformation.

The belief in the possibility of transformation is what makes it possible to work at change, and see it blocked, and still go on—because transformation does happen. It is easiest to see in individuals who, suddenly or slowly, discover newness in themselves and seem to be different people in small ways or great ones—and yet that hope and energy and generosity were always there, only waiting to be unblocked.

It happens politically too, as groups of people, even nations, learn to take on their own future. As with individuals the process is flawed. Social transformation is wonderful but messy, it can be hijacked by greedy people or greedy corporations or greedy neighbor-nations, but the fact that it happens at all is amazing. Very poor people have often not only been kept in poverty for others' profit, but told—generation after generation—that it is God's will and unalterable; yet a new knowledge can grow, and a new hope, and the ability to organize and sacrifice for change suddenly emerges, because it was always there, as a seed survives in dry ground until one day the rain comes and the seed sprouts and grows and flowers.

Transformation is part of the nature of reality because nothing is static; change goes on all the time, in people and plants and rivers and mountains and society. Change can be so slow that nobody notices, and it is easy to feel we can keep things the way they have been, especially if the way they have been is comfortable and profitable for the particular group of people to which we happen to belong.

But change will happen anyway. If we try to block it too long, it will happen explosively, as when the earth's tectonic plates, slowly pushing against each other, suddenly are pushed upwards by the resistance and the result is an earthquake. An earthquake is a disaster for people, because we choose to live as if it could not happen, but in itself an earthquake is just the way the earth changes. Those who have an interest in keeping things more or less the same and ignoring the human cost (which is most of the middle-class northern/western people) can block change that might increase their taxes or reduce their standard of living, but we have to know that some time something will break: maybe the market, maybe the social structures that keep people poor so that some may continue to be rich and richer, maybe the political structures that legislate to support the profits of rich corporations and ignore the needs of people and environments. It has happened before. When pressure is great enough the explosion happens—but it isn't necessarily violent in the sense of involving war and bloodshed. Most people think of political or social transformation as necessarily violent, because that is how we have been taught to think, so that we won't have sympathy with anyone who challenges the existing system. Whenever protesters gather to oppose injustice or defend the earth, the media focus exclusively on the few who use the occasion to turn violent (are often deliberately provoked into violence) partly because violence makes for better headlines but also because those who own our newspapers and TV networks don't want us to recognize that the tens of thousands of peaceful demonstrators and the millions behind them who felt the same way are a serious challenge to the current distribution of power. But real social and political transformation has been most effective when it was not violent, but was simply the refusal of ordinary people to cooperate with oppression. It worked in India when Gandhi led the movement that defeated the well-armed might of the British Empire (and helped to end the Empire, too). It happened in South Africa when white dominance and apartheid were ended without the bloodbath that had been predicted by those who hoped to discourage support for the struggle. It happened in Nazi-occupied Denmark, when the quiet non-cooperation of factory workers and of the whole population made Denmark useless to the German war machine. It happened when Polish shipyard workers brought about the downfall of the Communist regime and, not long after, it happened when the Berlin Wall came down. It happened in Chile, at great cost, when eventually the well-armed and ruthless Pinochet regime collapsed in the face of popular will. The civil rights movement in the U.S. was such a movement. None of these transformations was without cost, and often the cost was high, in terms of imprisonment, even many deaths. But the violence was that of those who refused to change. We see it every time a peaceful demonstration is met by heavily armed police or soldiers, as well as in places where any dissent is met with terror and death.

In our world, now, there are signs of impending earthquake, certainly literal ones, but a metaphorical social and political earthquake may come too. When it comes, as in the past, those who live over the fault—governments and the corporations that run them—experience this as disaster. For those who are willing to imagine and work and sacrifice and care, it can be transformation.

Yet transformation is not the end but the beginning. It is vulnerable, dangerous, frightening. It is the moment at which much can go wrong, but all kinds of people and places can recover beauty and compassion and efficiency (the real kind) and hope.

Eternal Life

*E*ternal doesn't mean going on forever and ever because "going on" is a time idea—one thing after another—and "eternal" means there's no time. We can't imagine it, and it can't help sounding a bit bleak. Even adding "life" to the idea simply means we rely on images of life as we know it, meaning it does go "on," events succeeding each other, perhaps wonderful ones. But we know, really, if reluctantly, that "eternal" cancels all our images.

What is left? Eternity, no beginning or end or middle—nothing? Emptiness? But a Hebrew psalm says, "With an *eternal* love you have loved us." Eternal, empty of time, of event—but love? The thought that comes through is that eternity is emptiness because it is boundless capacity; it is nothing because it contains all possibility. The non-event of eternity is that from which all events explode. The emptiness of eternity is absolute fullness. It is called "love" because eternity—nothing, the timeless, the shapeless, the image-less—is the womb from which come all times, all shapes, all images. They are not distinct from that eternal life, they are *made* of it, they are *in* it.

Buddhism speaks of the material world as "illusion." I used to think that Buddhists thought all the beauty and passion and life didn't really exist, that it was all just a fantasy. But the "illusion" is simply the conviction that we are *separate*, that the distinct reality of *things*, with their beauty or ugliness, their fragility, their possibility, exists only in separateness and so the only kind of permanence they can have is just to go on being like that as long as possible. And all the time we know it won't go on, and so we grieve. "With an eternal love you have loved us" tells us that the separateness, the exact and wonderful distinctiveness and variety of life is cradled by eternity, the eternity by which it is manifested and from which it is never parted. Not "either-or" but "both-and."

If we realize that the most vibrant life we see or experience— the irrepressible verdancy of fields and forests, when plants return after fires and above ruins, the indomitable courage and optimism of children who continue to hope and grow even in inhuman conditions, the lunatic passions of lovers that have inspired stories, plays, music—that all this is simply what eternity (emptiness, nothing) *contains*, then we may have a hard time referring to this as "eternal life" because that somehow sounds so calm and unchanging. It is really more like a volcano; I've used that image before because, although it can seem too violent, at least it helps to rub out the calm and saintly sweet associations of "eternal life."

If eternal life is something we know, now, because it cradles us in such compassion, then what happens when we die? Do we meet again the people we loved? Or do we rejoin the "great soul" and let go of separateness? Separateness is our experience, it is how we know, love, how we *are*. What's left without that? Can we—not *imagine*, perhaps, but conceive the thought that we might rediscover the people, the places and things, and the desires and dreams that we loved, and also let go the separateness that made our love for them always painful as well as wonderful? If eternal life is that emptiness which is crammed with infinite possibility, like a seedpod ready to burst, then to become part of that emptiness is to *be* that fullness of possibility, which therefore contains all joy and beauty and amazement. I'm not sure if that is an acceptable description of heaven but anyway I find it quite attractive. I definitely believe in eternal life because it makes sense of so much of my experience and that of people I know and love.

There's another thing I think about when I think of eternal life, and that is the earth. That thought about earth is really contained in what I said already, but I think there is a special kind of grief that many of us feel at the terrible destruction which is being wrought on this fragile, incredibly beautiful planet. We wonder if it will recover, or if we are, not too slowly, destroying ourselves and the earth together. Maybe we are, or maybe the signs of awareness have not come too late and the human race will be converted and learn to live in interdependence with other kinds of life, and the mountains and rivers and seas. But whatever we do, in the long—very long—run, the earth will come to an end. I find it comforting, in a deep way, to recognize that eternal life has the same meaning for Gaia as for me. She emerged from that cradle of possibility and is eternally held by it like me.

Happiness

I used to think that happiness was a random event that happened to people at moments when everything was going well for them, or at special times like falling in love, or visiting a beautiful place with a person we love, or having a healthy baby, or coming home after a long absence. Happiness, I thought, was not only random but fairly rare, and certainly not to be counted on. When a friend asked me, "Are you happy?" I thought it (privately) a foolish question. I was even a bit annoyed by it. My annoyance was due, I realized, to the implication that I *ought* to be happy, and if I wasn't there must be something wrong with me! But what, after all, was there to feel happy about in a world full of terror, poverty and uncertainty—except at those unusual moments when personal delight overcame the gloom that was, possibly, more appropriate?

Are happy people simply blocking out the world's misery? Are they even deluding themselves about the precariousness of their own reasons for happiness?

In the end I discovered a different way of thinking about happiness. It took a long time of gradually learning to allow myself to be open to reality as a whole: neither the good nor the bad alone, but the inevitably interwoven nature of both. The joy of a child's laugh and the terrible vulnerability of children; the horror of war and the heights of heroism in it; the pain of illness and the courage and compassion it evokes; the delight of love and the precariousness of it. There is grief hurting in every joy, humiliation behind every achievement and, above all, endings waiting for every beginning. Nevertheless, there is hope surging beyond every failure, compassion and imagination to tackle every disaster. When a tree falls, insects and fungi flourish, and new seedlings grow to take up the space. In the ruins of bombed cities the rubble turns purple with the blazing fireweed.

Nothing lasts, neither evil nor good, but to realize this is not to settle for a resigned detachment. On the contrary, it means that what is good and strong and beautiful must be passionately cherished, loved, praised, wondered at, just because it is fragile and passing. It will pass, whether it be a wildflower or a great temple or a mountain or a human life, but that makes it all the more wonderful. A plastic rose, however red, does not give a message of love as does the rose that will fade and die— the ephemeral quality is partly what moves us. The tiny grief implicit in the beauty makes it more precious.

Conversely, the knowledge that what is evil also has an end gives the courage to fight against it, to try to give goodness and beauty a little longer, to create more space for joy to grow. And if death is the end, at least of the kind of life we know, then we want to cherish and protect that life and give it every chance to discover yet more unexpected loveliness.

So I've discovered that happiness is not the absence of pain or grief, one's own or other people's. It is not even, or not only, that flooding in of delight at something wonderful. Happiness is about knowing that this delight is part of reality, but that beyond and enwrapping the delight is compassion, which is the essential nature of reality. Happiness is being able to touch, at least a little, that reality at the heart of the world where nothing is everlasting but everything is precious. Only saints are in touch with that reality on a permanent basis—indeed I wonder if even saints manage it all the time. But anyone can choose to know that it is so.

P. S.

*F*or now, these are the gifts I choose. Writing about them has been illuminating for me, and exciting, because until I began to try to *name* some of the things that give me life and hope, weaving the gifts into what I called a wreath, I hadn't realized what an amazing gift each one is—and the weaving of them, connecting in odd and unexpected ways, doesn't just add them up, it multiplies them. The wreath seems to reach out beyond the gifts I've chosen and woven together, to encircle many things I can't fully understand.

I could go on—the gifts in my life are many more than these, and more than I can ever perceive and consciously choose. Also, apart from the fact that the book would be overloaded if I tried to include all I can think of (how about saints and bonfires and death and forgiveness and wood and water and hands and . . . and . . .), my purpose here is simply to acknowledge amazed gratitude in the face of this field of flowers which is my life, our life. So I would like to believe that some who have experienced the bitterness of spiritual alienation and emptiness might dare to think that perhaps they can discover among the ruins gifts of fantastic richness. These gifts are like flowers, obstinately and cheerfully growing in all the mess. The fragile wreath is so easy to make from those flowers. It may be clumsy, it is not expert, it is awesome and ordinary, the flowers are common and yet the whole is rarer than a necklace of pearls. It is easy to despise a thing so fragile, so ephemeral, but it is all we have, and it shines like the stars and is eternal.